The Jeubs don't do anything small. When they make a commitment they dive in and give it their best. As the committed parents of 15 children and with another on the way, Chris and Wendy have some wisdom that every parent needs to hear. The number of children we have is not what matters; knowing how to create an atmosphere of love and support to the children we have does matter. This family knows how to do that. I wish I had read this book 30 years ago. I would have been a better dad. I might have also had more children.

—Ken Davis
Ken Davis Productions

If you have a, shall we say, petite family like my wife and I do (one child and not really counting right now), you don't have to work very hard or think very long about your family decisions. You certainly don't have to try to persuade anybody else to follow your example. If you're at 15-going-on-16 children like the Jeubs, though, you are truly doing something that's worth sharing, worth trying to convince others that it's a joy to love another child. Chris and Wendy not only deserve the platform they've been given (through this book, online and on TV), they make great use of it, facing down the giants of fear, apathy and cultural coercion to shape their family the way God called them to shape it—in a word, LARGE!

—Steven Isaac
Colorado Springs

After having spent time with Chris, Wendy and the 13 youngest children as house guests, it is good to see them answer their critics. They are a blessed family! How precious that they "walk their talk" and that they have been blessed with yet another child to love. From watching the sibling interactions to the nightly prayer time where even the youngest Jeubs chime in on cue, Chris and Wendy are training and discipling their children on a daily basis. If you want to know how parents develop deep relationships with each child, just live with them for a few days and you will see how they capitalize on each child's strengths. God has blessed the Jeubs, and with His guidance, the arrows He has given them will fly straight and true when the time comes.

—Marie Stout
California Mom to Five Children

Chris and Wendy, with crystal clarity, articulate the joy and rewards of accepting more children as a blessing. The greatest factor in most couples' reluctance to love another child is fear. It is fear that holds most of us back. Not enough money... Not enough time... Can't give attention to so many children... What will my parents think?...How many children can my body stand? When you read *Love Another Child* you will learn courage and have peace.

—Ron and Ruth Stauffer
Colorado Parents to Nine Children

Every young couple should read this book and contemplate its personal, heartfelt, and love-filled message. Chris and Wendy are bold messengers of the truths about having children that modern society rejects. As a natural childbirth advocate, I also am glad for their voice for a healthy and normal view of childbirth.

—Jessica Hulin, CBE, CLD
www.joyfulbirths.com

I loved this book! This is much more than a story of embraced fertility; it is a story of a deep faith in God, personal faithfulness and friendship inside and outside of family, and forgiveness toward short-sighted foes. This book motivates and inspires!

—Patricia Byrnes
Anchor of Hope Ministries

If you are wondering if you could love another child, this thought provoking book is a must read! The Jeubs clearly explain why they welcome 16 children into their family. They confess that they are not supernaturally patient or extra-gifted at organization, and you don't have to be either! They are simply willing to let God's love and grace carry them through the journey of raising a large family.

—Connie, Mother of Eight
SmockityFrocks.com

The Jeubs remind us through their candid talk and insightful help what many have overlooked: Children are our priceless treasures. Choosing life is a lifestyle that embraces the treasures around your table. In spite of the culture's persuasions and economic fears, children are assets and our greatest resources to be cultivated in love. Chris and Wendy's casual way of writing makes you think you are sitting at their table over a cup of coffee as they pour into you their love for family and the challenge to love another child.

—Gail McWilliams
Author and Speaker
www.GailMcWilliams.com

Love Another Child

Children. They're blessings. Always.

Chris & Wendy Jeub

WestBow
PRESS
A DIVISION OF THOMAS NELSON

Scripture taken from the HOLY BIBLE, NEW INTERNATIONAL VERSION®. Copyright © 1973, 1978, 1984 Biblica. Used by permission of Zondervan. All rights reserved.

WestBow Press books may be ordered through booksellers or by contacting:

WestBow Press
A Division of Thomas Nelson
1663 Liberty Drive
Bloomington, IN 47403
www.westbowpress.com
1-(866) 928-1240

Cover Image Credit: Kim Harms Photography, http://www.kimharms.com

ISBN: 978-1-4497-1063-7 (sc)
ISBN: 978-1-4497-1065-1 (dj)
ISBN: 978-1-4497-1064-4 (e)

Library of Congress Control Number: 2010943068

Printed in the United States of America

WestBow Press rev. date: 1/17/2011

Contents

1 - Our Early Convictions

"The happiest moments of my life have been the few which I have passed at home in the bosom of my family." —Thomas Jefferson

Life at our home is never boring. Activity is the rule of our day, and we thrive on it. We're busy, but it isn't a dysfunctional brand of busy, like a workaholic who dives into his job to avoid deeper issues in life. We're busy because there is life going on in every corner of our house. Right now, the baby's starting to stand up, the toddler is into spontaneous dancing, the preschooler is reading the alphabet, the boys are growing like weeds and the teenagers are preparing for speech and debate tournaments. There is never a boring moment in our home. Children are our life, and *family* is who we are.

Perhaps this is what people find fascinating about big families like ours. Children are dynamic, full of unique personality. The social norm is approximately two children per couple, a nuclear family composed of, everyone hopes, one boy and one girl. I can imagine what they think of families like ours. "Wow, our family multiplied *eight* times. That's insane!" And they watch popular television shows about large families with extreme interest and curiosity.

We didn't have the benefit of popular shows about large families early in our married life. When Wendy and I were married, we wanted to have a family, but 15 children was never—*never!*—a consideration for us. Honestly, we had difficulty with the idea of letting our children come one after another, because no one in our social circles was doing anything close to what was on our hearts.

1

When we hit No. 5 (our first son, Isaiah), it was time to stop, it seemed. I (Chris) was a school teacher with more children at home than any of the other teachers in the entire district. Opinions rolled in—usually unsolicited—from doctors, co-workers, neighbors, church friends and extended family members. We didn't have a family of a dozen kids next door encouraging us to have another child. We were alone in our conviction.

On our hearts during those years was a simple prodding: *Have another child.* It wasn't "have 15 children" or "have more children than anyone else." Just *another.* Our conviction was, we had thought, unique from other couples. Our personal relationship with God was healthy, and this conviction—shaped for our lives and our hearts—was one we couldn't simply shake off. As husband and wife, we prayed and studied the Bible together. We reasoned through our weak moments when we doubted our calling and questioned our sanity.

And when serious doubts did creep into our minds, our fertility won out. Despite a fair amount of effort to avoid pregnancy, we proceeded to have three boys in a row: Isaiah was followed by Micah and Noah. Bing, bang, boom! There was hardly a year between any of them. So by 1998 we had seven children. We were still in our 20s. And we were feeling incredibly healthy and blessed.

A funny thing happened at seven children. The social pressure disappeared. Family and friends stopped dropping those annoying comments like, "Aren't you done yet?" or, "You do know how that happens, don't you?" When you have two, you're extremely normal; at four or five, you're in the same boat as many married couples, wondering whether or not to cut the line and stop having children. Once you're at seven, though, you're in Looneyland—you're "out there" and there ain't no persuadin' you.

Something happened to *us*, too. The pressures to conform began to roll off our backs. Instead of doubting our convictions, we would reflect on how great our life was. We laughed the wisecracks off. "You do know how that happens, don't you?" *Yes! And we're really good at it.* Here's one that I told a newspaper reporter, and it ended up in the local paper: *Wendy knows, but she won't tell me.* Even the most cynical laugh with us.

We're now in our 40s, have two adult children, two grandchildren, four teenagers, two tweenagers, three grade schoolers, two kindergartners, two toddlers ... and we're expecting our 16th child. We look back on our early 20s and think, *how petty our anxiousness was.* We wrung our hands and struggled with our convictions. For what? To avoid this life of limitless activity, joy and love? We are so happy we can hardly stand it. When we sit back and reflect (it rarely happens in our busy life, but we manage to find the time now and then), we are incredibly thankful that, when we were young, our faith triumphed over our doubt.

Perhaps this is why families find lives like ours fascinating: We are carefree about our reproductive lives, open to how God will plan our family, refusing to dwell on the negative point of view our culture delivers about children. We're still young—we will have more children, Lord willing—and we live a life free from the burden of worry that we may have another child. Controlling conception doesn't fill our thoughts and discovering a pregnancy is, without any hesitation, joyous news. We make love without worrying something will "go wrong." This freedom is wonderful. This family life is liberating.

Deep down, couples wonder, "What would our life be like if we just let children come?" Is the "dangerous" antithesis of family planning to live on the edge like the Jeubs? There is something underneath the fascination and curiosity. Is it envy? Regret? Does the normal couple who birthed the average family, got the vasectomy or tubal ligation, and had the "perfect societal family" ever stop and wonder what it would have been like with a dozen or so children running around the house? Or at least one or two more than they had?

Consider some of the criticism large families receive. Our hate-mail folder is full of cruel messages from people who think we're beyond crazy, maybe even a little evil:

- "People like you having more kids than the planet can handle are running the country into the ground. Sucking our resources dry. And for what? To glorify yourselves."
- "You will probably delete this comment, but this honestly sounds like your delusional way to justify your large family's enormous carbon footprint on our planet."
- "NUTS. You're nuts. Thought about buying your cookbook but can't support your crazy ideas. I'll go elsewhere for my cookbook. Sorry."
- "Good luck taking over the world with your army of babies. I don't think God would approve of using children as a weapon. Children need individual attention and love. How is that possible with nearly 20 kids? Please enlighten me if you can. But this cult is sounding more and more like the Taliban every day!"

Does it really sound like *we're* the dysfunctional ones here? There's something hidden underneath messages like these, as there always is under this kind of rage. Strip the outer layer away and you often see regret and pain, perhaps a personal struggle with a conviction similar to ours. Early in our parenting lives we might have responded similarly. I don't think we would have been quite so rash, but we certainly could have mustered a fair amount of defensiveness and perhaps even anger. Such responses would have reflected an inner doubt of our own, and instead of dealing with it maturely, with intellectual conversation, we would have grown agitated.

Case in point: 1993. The Minnesota Pro-life Action League published an article written by a pro-life activist. The article claimed that avoiding conception was a sin, that the Bible's mandate to "be fruitful and multiply" was never rescinded and that Natural Family Planning (NFP) was, indeed, just as bad as being pro-choice.

At the time, we had just finished our NFP classes, and we were *at least trying* not to conceive children. You can see how this article got under our skin. Who did this guy think he was? He was comparing our responsible parenting decisions to pro-abortion activists. We wrote a scathing letter to the editor, ripping the publication's poor editorial choice. We flexed every rhetorical muscle we had to make sure such a vile opinion would never be published again. The result?

We received a letter of apology from the editor, and the sequels of this article were never published.

Granted, the author erred when comparing family planning— any family planning—to abortion. We zeroed in on this error and made it our biggest issue. But it was his other not-so-radical point that was the true source of our wild reaction: God had a plan for our family, and He had plans for our children who were not yet born. Many Christian parents wrestle with this conviction, just as we did in 1993, and this article served as an uncomfortable reminder.

We're embarrassed today to tell you that story. The good folks who pour themselves into the abolition of abortion deserve our support, not our attacks. The author held a different, stronger opinion than ours, but we should have been fine with that. We didn't believe—and still don't today—that couples who practice non-abortive birth control are necessarily "living in sin," as this author stated. However, how many couples can claim their practice is a *conviction,* that God is calling them to *avoid* another child? We don't know many.

Over the years, our desire has turned into encouraging couples who share in our original conviction, the conviction we had thought was unique to us. We're not big into condemning others for their choices. We have several friends, in fact, who do not subscribe to some of ours. But having children is one of those biggies in life that couples should consider seriously—and the earlier the better. So we're becoming more and more vocal about how our personal convictions make a tremendous amount of sense. Our "live and let live" motto has changed to a more direct, "Are you sure you want to live that way?" We talk with several 40-somethings who regret either pushing children late into their lives or cutting off their childbearing years early. They're older, they get tired, and their 20s can't be relived. These folks are the ones to whom young parents should listen when they say, "We sure wish we had children in our 20s rather than waiting so long." Seldom (never?) do we hear regrets from those who did have children while young.

We've decided we need to push a little harder when we meet 20-somethings who instinctively blow off the advice of their elders.

We want to prolong the conversation with those who hear our message of *Love Another Child* and laugh it off—or grow angry with it, like some of those whose letters end up in our hate-mail folder. It is much easier to flow with the popular culture which encourages young people to have as few children as possible, maybe even *none*. If you are in your 20s, turn your ears toward your elders who share with you their regrets. You'll find that they never regret the travel, material possessions or career opportunities that family life inevitably restricts. Instead, they regret their preconceived notions that kept them from having, raising and loving children.

What to Envy

Early in our marriage when we had only three children, we hosted a Bible study in our St. Cloud, Minn., apartment. We had envisioned hosting a study with couples our age, so we invited couples from our homeschool group. It was a surprise, then, when Jim and Nancy showed up. We were in our 20s; Jim and Nancy were pushing 50. We were as poor as hillbillies; they were quite wealthy. I (Chris) was just graduating from college with a teaching degree while Wendy worked to get me through; Jim owned a million-dollar real estate business for which Nancy was the manager. We were stepping into the working world; Jim and Nancy were looking to sell their business and retire early.

Wendy was pregnant with our fourth child, and our eldest, Alicia, was old enough to babysit all the kids who came to the study with their parents, while the adults were in the living room. And I should note that Jim and Nancy were blessed with one "accidental" child they had in their late 40s. But we still sort of wondered why they wanted to be in our study.

I remember one evening sitting in the living room before the rest of the group arrived. Wendy and Nancy were situating the kids with a video. I was prodding Jim with praise for his financial success: "You really played your cards right"; "Maybe I should invest in real estate"; "I admire people like you." I was so optimistic, so naive.

Jim stopped me cold with the straight composure of an experienced financial planner. "Chris, don't envy me. I would give it all up to have six teenagers running around my house right now." He then proceeded to tell me how *he* envied *me* for having children in my early years. It's safe to say Jim's advice settled into my heart. Point taken: On the other side of my 20s, 30s and 40s, I won't measure prosperity by my bank account; I'll measure it by my heritage of children.

Don't think, though, that bearing your own children is the only way to build toward that heritage. Adoptions are equal in every way. Wendy and I married as a blended family (Wendy was a single mom with two children), and adoptions made us an immediate family of four. People have, now and then, made inconsiderate remarks about how our relationships with our adopted children are somehow inferior to the relationships we have with the children we have birthed together. But there is no "step" in our family. There is no distance caused by the gift of adoption.

We make the argument that the Bible calls us to welcome the blessing of children, and we extrapolate from that mandate some opinions about birth control. While there is room for disagreement over our interpretation of the Bible in regard to birth control, there is no room for disagreement over adoption. James 1:27 couldn't be more direct: "Religion that God our Father accepts as pure and faultless is this: to look after orphans and widows in their distress." Parents who voluntarily take in children with no parents of their own are—in God's perspective—living a pure and faultless faith.

Children are a heritage of the Lord's. Period. Adopted and blood-related alike. We believe the conviction to seek the orphans and adopt them is just as strong today as the conviction to allow God to bless you with children who are genetically linked to you. Perhaps this is an awakening of God's people, to embrace the heritage of children, to "be fruitful and multiply." We know several families who embrace adoption of children from other countries and through the foster care system in our own country, and, like us, the blessings abound from their original conviction. It's beautiful, definitely "pure and faultless," exciting and adventurous to say the least.

The days and years go by, and before you know it, you're past your reproductive years. Some couples panic and manage to conceive one child as the clock ticks loudest, and that one child invariably brings an overwhelming realization: *What have we been doing the last two decades?* All your travel, career-building and, yes, even partying pales in comparison to having children. The scales fall from your eyes and you see profound love unlike any previous ambition. Some adopt. And the blessings flow from there. We know couples who have done this, and they are loving—albeit later in life—the exciting life of parenting.

Wendy and I are now sitting on the other end of our most productive years. We try to stay healthy and fit, but the 40s work against you. We're more tired today; we look back on the energy of our 20s and think about how we took our youth for granted. But in terms of having children, we have no regrets. Since our marriage in 1991 we have lived one year at a time, most of those years on the cutting edge of our paychecks, receiving children as they've come. God has always provided. And now, young couples in our community and through our website seek our advice often. We always encourage them to seek God in their marriage and welcome with open arms and hearts the prospect of children.

Those who embrace their convictions should be encouraged to know that they won't be in their 20s forever, and that their house full of little ones will not always be so overwhelming. When the house is a mess and the kids are acting up, moms can think of Wendy taking care of a much larger household. When the finances are tight and the business prospects thin, dads can take Chris' work ethic to heart and press on to provide for their family. Family is too powerful a thing to ever take for granted—or regret.

And that's why our encouragement folder is much thicker than our hate-mail folder. Here are a few from couples who read our blog and our books:

- "We were once scared about the prospect of a lot of kids, but now we are excited about it. It is definitely freeing, as well, to not have to 'plan' your family. We are thankful for your family and the ministry you have in encouraging others. Please keep it up."

- "What will the future bring? I don't know. But this I do … God will always be there for us and guide our steps as we serve Him. We are not better than others with a smaller number of children, but we experience the blessing and peace of having what God has given to us, with an open heart."

- "We've gone back and forth on the idea of how many children to have and had decided for three years that our little girl would be our only child. And then after a couple of years of reading your blog and watching the shows, we decided to just let it happen. I'm 9 weeks along with our second child and I am almost in tears [with thankfulness]. It's so selfless to give your lives to God and just take each child as they come. … I'm so relieved that we have decided to just let God take over."

- "Something my husband and I have always tried to do is be a living testimony of the joy and delight of a larger-than-average family (six children with us). That's one thing I've appreciated about you folks, too. Simply living life together, fully trusting God for the future, whatever it may hold."

- "Do you realize what an inspiration you are to people? Thank you for stepping out there and trusting God, and telling your story no matter whether you get criticized for obeying your convictions. Amazing. We are parents to nine beautiful blessings and have struggled through the years with giving our fertility wholly to the Lord. But when we really think about it, how can we not? How can we ask God to bless us with a new home or new car or whatever else to provide for our daily needs and then turn around and say, 'But please don't bless me with more children'?"

These moms and dads *get it*. They understand what we're saying: Children are a heritage from heaven, gifts from God, and families who treat them as such are in for a fantastic life. Standing on this side of our productive years, free from the fear of the unknown, of what parenting will be like, we wouldn't trade it for anything. We don't regret having any of our 15 children. And we can't wait for the 16th!

The Most Excellent Way

We do have this regret: We wish we'd understood the profundity of love at a younger age. Without love, having children is just a legalistic command from the Bible. We urge much more than to just *have* another child. We encourage families to *Love Another Child*, and for good reason. If we could have had that mom and dad of a dozen kids next door pour their wisdom on us when we were young and struggling with our convictions, we imagine them telling us to love our children *even more.*

This is the greater error young families make, greater than the decision to cut off children altogether. Our hearts are heavy for families who choose to center on perfect behavior, perfect dress, perfect homeschool, perfect everything. We're not impressed. We've witnessed homes that are heralded as perfect families, but they're in turmoil because of a profound lack of love in the marriage and for their children. Likewise, we've witnessed homes with few children—maybe even parents who think we're nuts and have therefore embraced birth control—where love abounds. Love is what makes these households fulfilled. Love is the centerpiece to a family's relationship with God and with one another.

This lines up perfectly with God's Word. Some may disagree with our views on what the Scriptures say about birth control, and, to be honest, that's fine with us. We can still be friends. But about love? If you disagree with us on love, you've got issues, and we likely won't get along very well. The Bible is full of references to love. And it's not only referenced, it is deemed the "most excellent way" and the "greatest commandment." *Love is it,* the big kahuna of life. Children are a great blessing, but take love from that blessing and you're left with turmoil and dysfunction.

Love—or the lack of it—is the root of the rage found in our hate-mail folder. People point to our children and seem to get hot and bothered, but if they were to hang out with us for a few days, they'd come to see that their prejudices aren't justified. Chances are good that those who lash out at us are struggling with a dysfunctional view of love—a view that likely started from their own family upbringing. They are hurt, and *hurting people hurt people.* The answers they're looking for won't be found in rage or judgment, but in the love that comes from a living God.

This was the realization that we wrote about in our first book, *Love in the House.* After three painful years of separation from our oldest child, we walked through reconciliation that revealed a deficit of love in our family. For years we had walked in faith; it wasn't as if our house was void of love, but our perspective of the importance of love was cockeyed, off target. Parents of prodigal children often learn this perspective, sadly late in life. Standing on this side of 20-plus years of raising children, we've got some profound things to say about "love in the house."

So a follow-up book was definitely in order. And we've titled it with a motto we've latched onto that sums it all up: *Love Another Child*. If you are able to *love another child,* there is nothing holding you back from an exciting family life, even one with many children. There is nothing wrong with such a worthy aspiration. In fact, there is *everything right* about it. Your conviction to love another child is one we share with you, and we are certain you will not regret walking in your conviction.

2 - The Camera's Eye

"We cannot solve all the problems in the world, but let us never bring in the worst problem of all, and that is to destroy love." — *Mother Teresa*

A Facebook friend was contacted by CNN to do a show on the so-called "Quiverfull Movement." Before committing she contacted us to ask of our experience with TLC, Reuters, CBS and other media opportunities we've had. Our e-mail conversation revealed horrific, out-of-the-ordinary details of her life. One son was killed in a car accident, another ran away from home. Her daughter was calling the police on them. Clearly, her life was falling apart, and CNN appeared to be seeking to expose darkness lurking in large families. We advised her not to do the show.

We were on TLC (formerly The Learning Channel) in 2007 in the miniseries *Kids by the Dozen*. The show featured the lives of unusually large families like our own. The crew consisted of an onsite producer, an assistant producer, a cameraman and a soundman who visited our home for an eight-day stretch of interviewing and filming. They followed up with our oldest daughter for a couple more days of filming, plus several phone conversations with studio editors and producers based in New York.

It was a good experience. Even though the cameras exposed an uncomfortable situation (that of our prodigal relationship with our daughter Alicia), the story unfolded quite fairly and accurately. In the end, it became a beautiful story of love in our home (hence the name of our preceding book *Love in the House*), a story that unfolded largely because of the fact that cameras were rolling. Like it or not, TLC wanted the truth, we signed the contract, and we felt we needed to be honest about it.

The show spread nationally and is sometimes shown internationally. We get all sorts of comments on our website whenever our show is broadcast. The experience placed us onto a platform from which we can now speak to the issue of large-family living. We've welcomed the opportunity. If you were to sum up our public life, I suppose it would be much like this: We're followers of Christ who were convicted early in our marriage to have children—to allow God to continue to bless us with them—and we've experienced great joy mixed with our share of challenges. Like it or not, this is our life, and we're quite honest about it.

Judging from the success of the show, most people respect our convictions. But there are others who don't. In fact, some folks love to hate them. We were shocked at first by how cruel people could be toward large families, and it took some getting used to. There are television gossip sites filled with users outraged at our audacity to have so many children. After viewing 46 running minutes of our lives, some viewers blasted their judgment all over the Internet. Not just at us, either, but at all the families on the *Kids by the Dozen* show—as well as others on TLC.[1]

There were some sheepish moments of doubt, wondering if we should be so transparent. Really, we've got children to raise and a life to live. The camera complicates things. We feared that our decision to open our lives to the camera's eye was a mistake. This fear was short-lived, though, primarily because of our faith in God's calling for us. We're quite certain of our walk of faith, and we grow more and more confident as our life unfolds. Just like our having children, sometimes we fear we are not making the right choices, but we remind ourselves that God is in control, and He led us in this direction. The results are in His hands, and we are constantly amazed at how things work out.[2]

We believe our perspective on children is somewhat unique today. Children are a blessing to their families, to their world. They are a true heritage. They are not annoying liabilities to our lives, as adversaries to having children attempt to portray them. Children are a blessing from God, no more complex than that, so no wonder we agree with Psalm 127, which ends with, "Blessed is the man who has his quiver full of them."

But back to those who would oppose us: There is an opposition to families like ours, an adversary more articulate than those who spew venom on gossip sites. Our second big television opportunity (though not nearly as big as the first) gave this opposition a voice. We were approached by CBS News and were pitched this idea: A camera crew would come to film us for a day or two while producers would visit and interview us. Compared to TLC's grueling two weeks, this seemed like a cinch. We signed with CBS News and proceeded. The filming went great, we had a lot of fun with the producers and camera crew, and we expected another TLC-style exposé on the Jeubs.[3]

We'd been told the show would be called "Quiverfull Mothers" and be a documentary on CBS News. But it wound up on the Women's Entertainment Network (WE tv). The series that featured us (and two other Quiverfull families) was *Secret Lives of Women*. Our episode was titled "Born to Breed."

Secret lives? Nothing secret about our lives. What's with the title? *Born to Breed?*

One of the other two mothers interviewed became an advocate *against* families like ours. An investigative journalist was consulted, too, and given center stage as "the expert" on families with many children.

We researched past episodes of *Secret Lives of Women*. Polygamists, abusive women, wives-gone-gay, pornographers and, believe it or not, *worse*. Its opening featured lap dancers and women in leather and whips, as if all women secretly desired sensuous night lives. We looked up the so-called expert who would tie the show together. A 30-year-old single woman with no children, she wrote a scathing article in *Newsweek* branding families like ours as Neanderthals. She also wrote a book where she attacked hardworking moms and dads and warned her readers to stay away from people like us.

The first preview was released two weeks before the show aired. Sinister music played in the background as a narrator explained what our lives were like. Wendy was quoted, largely out of context, saying, "Fifteen children is not enough!" In the interview, Wendy answered the question, "Do you feel like today you're missing out on anything?" In context, Wendy explained that she, in the past, had two children and felt like she was done. Now, with 15, she felt so overwhelmingly blessed, *it seems like* "15 children is not enough."

That's television for you. The good, the bad and the really ugly. This was a rough crowd we'd been thrown into. And it was an unpredictable crowd, too. TLC treated us right. It appeared CBS had a different approach.

We pray over every single media opportunity we have, and the CBS/WE opportunity seemed to open up quite naturally, as if God was blessing it. We'd turned down opportunities before, even some that promised large compensation. We interviewed with the CBS producers and were convinced that they were genuine, honestly seeking answers to our unique lifestyle. We don't doubt they were interested; we know we live an unusual life and that people are genuinely curious about our family. But "Born to Breed"? Seriously? We grew worried at how we would be portrayed, but by then there was nothing we could do. Besides, our faith, not our doubt, directs our steps. God opened this door for us, so no matter what happened—ridicule and shame included—we were going through with it.

Turns out the show wasn't half bad. The camera's eye captured the Jeub family in their element. While I (Chris) was present and included, Wendy was the star of the show. She beamed on camera, and CBS let us promote her new weight-loss book, *Love in a Diet*. She blew every stereotype of what women with 15 children should look like. Her first cookbook, *Love in the Kitchen*, was given front-and-center exposure as she explained how we cook and shop for our big family. Frugality, too, was brought to the fore, and I got to explain how our family business runs and how the older children are involved.

Viewers expected to see conformists, religious zealots. We laughed at the parts of the episode that showed "experts" (no doubt those who had no children of their own) talking about how fundamentalist and controlling we all were, painting a broad, judgmental picture. The camera then snapped to images of us living out values that are quite the opposite. Rachel Scott, a mother of eight who was also featured on the show, came across as a delightful and joyful mother, full of love. Rachel and Wendy are well-versed women of faith, both of them about as far from legalistic, dogmatic mothers as you'll find.

So if CBS intended for us to be made the fools, the plan backfired. Our story was a strong one, strong enough to push away the salacious trappings of *Secret Lives of Women*. God laid it on our hearts to have children, and we raise them with the tools He provides. Our "dicey" side is merely this: We push back on popular assumptions about families like ours. Wendy, especially, brings this message home to women.

Women like Wendy (housewife, mother of 15, living on a modest income) are constantly stereotyped. She should be fat, barefoot and pathetically pregnant, at her wits' end. Her life should be oppressive and overwhelming. She should have no self-esteem, no joy or fulfillment. She should be living in a shoe, for all the rest of the world knows.

The real Wendy—a fulfilled woman who follows the heartfelt conviction from God to have and bear children—dispels these myths. Come to think of it, this is a "secret life," one worth exposing on sensational television. We are a large, happy family living the life we were born to live.

The show brought to the surface a universal question women have: *What would my life be like if I, too, had children? Maybe a lot of children?* It gave everyone involved an opportunity to articulate their beliefs. Sure, it gave some a platform to sell their secular sneering. We believe most people saw through this. Criticism of couples who are merely responding to the calling to love another child is unfair, and in this show's case even hostile. These critics have run roughshod over the term Quiverfull (a term alluding to Psalm 127 and loosely used among professing Christians in the past 10-15 years) intentionally perverting it. They narrowly define the term with an ulterior motive: to take aim at religion, people of faith and parents who feel the conviction to have another child. It is brutally judgmental to take aim at moms and dads who are genuinely attempting to build their families. They point their fingers and condemn families that view children as blessings from God. That's their platform.

The show gave us a platform, too, an opportunity for rebuttal and explanation. While our opponents *told* everyone who they thought we were, we *showed* them who we really are. They were haughty and judgmental; we were simply ourselves. They shot a thin laser beam at how out-of-the-ordinary we were (one clip showed a critic calling large families "freaks"); we lit up the whole room with how we were people of faith and out-of-the-box thinkers. Showing, not telling, wins in the arena of persuasion, and we think most viewers weren't fooled.

What We Mean by "Quiverfull"

The show helped launch the term *Quiverfull* into the mainstream culture, a label we have always been a little wary of. The word *quiverfull*, like many words, come loaded with connotation. Deep words like *Christian* or *love* seldom do their meanings justice. They are better understood by observing, not defining. *Quiverfull* is another one of those words.

The term comes from one of the most poetic books of the Bible, the Psalms (or "Songs of God"). The subtitle in the header of our website is taken from the same Psalm and is a reference to the Quiverfull idea: "Children are a blessing of the Lord's." Here are the verses in full:

1 Unless the LORD builds the house,
  its builders labor in vain.
  Unless the LORD watches over the city,
  the watchmen stand guard in vain.
2 In vain you rise early
  and stay up late,
  toiling for food to eat—
  for he grants sleep to those he loves.
3 Sons are a heritage from the LORD,
  children a reward from him.
4 Like arrows in the hands of a warrior
  are sons born in one's youth.
5 Blessed is the man
  whose quiver is full of them.
  They will not be put to shame
  when they contend with their enemies in the gate.

One of the shortest chapters in the Bible, but one of the most poetic. Poetry, as defined by an English professor we once knew, is "condensed thoughts." We have found these verses to be incredibly encouraging as we walk in faith in what God is calling us to do. These verses validate our risks, galvanize our trust. We've applied them to our actions, and we can honestly attest that they have led to grand adventure.

A small side note on that: Many of the more profound verses in Scripture are misunderstood and often avoided. This is too bad, really. Naturally, cynics struggle with these "condensed thoughts." They may find large families interesting, but the real depth and understanding comes in *applying* the principles, not just discussing them. These are verses of faith, of walking the walk. We are people of faith and, truthfully, we can't imagine applying these verses without a solid faith.

Consider these words again, carefully, and how they apply to your life.

> Unless the LORD builds the house, its builders labor in vain.
> Unless the LORD watches over the city, the watchmen stand guard in vain.
> In vain you rise early and stay up late, toiling for food to eat—for he grants sleep to those he loves.

The metaphors of the first two stanzas illustrate that the psalmist wants us to put God in control of our family. Our home is our heritage, our family, the thing that matters most. We could have built our family without God in our life, but we would have done a lousy job. Like any family, we've turned to and fro through the exciting challenges of parenting and raising children. But for us, we have our faith guiding every step of the way.

Surrendering your life to God isn't the easiest thing to do. To atheists, it appears to be lunacy. Even to those of us who believe, it is a daring adventure. We have seen miracles happen in areas of our life that we would have otherwise thought hopeless. When you surrender your financial life to God, you might expect poverty, but we have been blessed with much more than monetary wealth. When you trust God with your employment, you may just receive the joy of self-employment. When you give your relationships to God, you might rear rejection, but we have discovered profound love. An atheist sees these steps like the blind man walking unaided, filled with hazard and desperate consequence. It's quite the contrary for those with faith; the consequences are wonderful. We've found this to be the way God works with us: *He wants our faith, then He takes care of the results.*

The same goes for our reproductive lives. We believe God wants us to trust Him in our family planning. To let Him take care of the results. We're more than fine with that. In fact, we are *amazed* at how incredible the blessings have been. We almost have to pinch ourselves to make sure we're not dreaming. We have 13 of our 15 children living in our home right now. Our dinnertime is packed with excitement and conversation. Our lives are never boring and constantly filled with action. To some, this is chaos and disorder. We think, *Can life be any better?*

The remaining verses challenge us to rethink how we see children.

> Sons are a heritage from the LORD, children a reward from him.

How have modern couples gotten it into their minds that children *aren't* a blessing? Few would be quite so blunt, but their actions sure show it. We've witnessed parents rant and rave on how difficult parenting is—while in earshot of their children. In our book *Love in the House,* I (Chris) tell of a mom who tried to convince a couple of snowboarders how awful parenting is:

> I recall sitting with three of our kids on a shuttle bus at a ski resort in Colorado when a mother sitting with two children struck up a conversation with a couple of college-aged men. This mother (within earshot of her kids) proclaimed: "Enjoy your life while you can! Once you have children, everything gets so difficult. What I would give to be young again!"
>
> I remember this so well because the two students—whom you might expect to chime right in and complain about children—brushed off this mother's advice. One long-haired snowboarder said, "I believe children are a blessing." His friend agreed, "Yeah, I look forward to having a family." So much for stereotypes.

This gets a little dicey when we challenge parents to rethink what they've been told all their lives: "Have perhaps one or two children, but then stop." Having more is seen as selfish or irresponsible. Like the mother on the bus, the "joys" of youth were much more desirable than the "agony" of parenting. Why, then, should one add to the pain by having *more* children?

These same parents would never admit that their one or two children aren't blessings. Even this mother on the bus—if pressed—would have admitted that she loved her children. Why, then, would you predetermine the *next* child to be some sort of curse?

Imagine for a moment you and God having a conversation. God says, "I want to bless you with $15 million." You return, "No thanks, God. Sounds like agony to me. I'll just put up with the few bucks I can manage on my own."

We'll take the $15 million, thank you very much. God's result? Our life is really, really good. It hasn't all been peachy, but who can claim a life that is? We can't imagine life without any one of our children, and now grandchildren. God had a fantastic plan in store for us when he laid on our hearts to let Him have control of our blessings. So the idea that any of our children are *not* blessings is ridiculous. Worse, it's kind of sinister. And that's why we take this concept a step further. We have 15 children, but why would we say that No. 16 won't be a blessing? Or 17? Or 18?

Let's rewind time and put some names to this idea. When we had Isaiah 14 years ago (our first son and fifth child), the conventional logic was to stop already! We had four daughters and now a son, why go on? But if we would have followed this course, we wouldn't have Micah, Noah, Tabitha, Keilah, Hannah, Josiah, Havilah, Joshua, Priscilla or Zechariah. People give us all sorts of reasons why they stopped having children, and very, very few include, "God told me to stop." Most often it's, "I couldn't handle any more children," "What would my in-laws think?" "I can't afford it," and so on. In other words, "Another child would not be a blessing."

These are fallacies, false dilemmas brewed up in our fallible minds. Verse 3 nips this in the bud, and from the remaining text blossoms the Quiverfull metaphor.

> Like arrows in the hands of a warrior are sons born in one's youth.

> Blessed is the man whose quiver is full of them. They will not be put to shame when they contend with their enemies in the gate.

These lines are written with military terms (arrows, warrior, quiver, enemies) to create a metaphor representing our walk through life. Whatever life throws at you, a solid family brings strength, stability and preparedness. Paraphrase: "As a warrior entering a battle with a quiver full of arrows, so are parents with a houseful of children." Whatever the enemy throws at your family, you can withstand it.

People often err in thinking of Quiverfull as some contest to have as many children as possible. We know Quiverfull-minded people with just a couple kids; they are content with their two and they are fine if God gives them more. Likewise, we have corrected people who cry out to God for as many children as the Jeubs. Because that is not the Quiverfull promise. We're not on a racetrack; we are merely letting God have control of our family's numbers. This is a walk of faith, not a casino game with hopes to cash in big.

You see, having a "full" quiver is a relative term. That could be 16 children for Chris and Wendy Jeub. It could be *one* for you. We're not out to manipulate the number, just accept it. This area of our life—that of so-called family planning—is in God's hands. We're pushing away the popular opinion that we should control that. Look at it this way: God is telling us to allow children to come naturally; the world tells us to artificially restrict their arrival. We go with God.

How freeing this walk is. It really is! We have been so blessed by our children, our extended family has been blessed, our children bless each other. There is so much blessing going around we can barely stand it! This is freedom, a good life, an abundant life.

The Movement to Build Loving Families

Every movement that pushes against the tide of the status quo will have its failures. Frail attempts at religious perfection is one such failure. And in the Quiverfull arena, all is not well all of the time. We are saddened when we witness a separation or divorce within a large family. Life could have been so much more grand for their beautiful—now broken—family.

It would be nice to have role models whom we could follow confidently down a wide and well-traveled path. The truth is that this path of childbearing has been suppressed for a few generations now, and those who walk down it are having to plow through some thick brush. Mistakes will be made along the journey, no doubt the legalism of the Quiverfull message carrying some of the blame. Keep in mind, though, that these most recent attacks aren't attacks against moms and dads desiring to love another child. They are attacks against folks who may have erred in judgment along the path God called them down.

What is our alternative, though? The world's idea of family? The world is fallen, ugly and separated from God. Is it sane to choose the "normal" path, conforming to expectations the world places in front of you? Shake that thought from your mind. God is calling you and millions of other moms and dads to something higher. Sure, you're going to get raised eyebrows from folks who neither understand nor care to try. Get used to it. That's the world. It's crazy and cruel and relentless. Thank God that you're just in it and not of it.

We stand resolved: We must continue to keep our hearts on what God has in store for us. Examples of failure do not threaten what God has laid on our heart, nor do the world's attempts to ridicule or criticize our choices. God has His heart on us, and we have our heart on Him. In love, we'll move forward with confidence.

And so should you. Pray earnestly and let God place on your heart what is best for your family. Move forward with faith, and let God handle the results. If that means another child, don't let contrary ideas worm their way into your decisions. You'll discover a freedom in Christ that is full of joy and blessing. And, perhaps, children.

---

3 - Financially Speaking

"I asked for riches that I might be happy. I was given poverty that I might be wise. ... I am, among all men, most richly blessed." —Unanswered Prayers

When working at Focus on the Family, I (Chris) republished an article online about the psychological harms of day care. The article, "The Truth About Day Care," came from Prison Fellowship and the office of Chuck Colson, respected Christian leader and cultural spokesperson. It passed our editorial standards and was not—contrary to what it seemed at first glance—a slam on parents who place their children in day care. With a great deal of factual support and clear rhetoric, the article made the claim that children raised by a parent at home fared much better than children placed in day care. This fact is largely undisputed, but still irritates parents who have their children in day care.

A mother in a separate department at Focus had a huge problem with the article, and she came to visit me about it. She was not too much younger than me, in her late 20s perhaps; she was dressed professionally and wore a modest wedding ring as she stood in my cubicle. "I have a problem with the tone of the article," she said. "It does not show both sides of the issue."

I knew exactly what she meant when she said it. When people complain about "the tone" of writing, it often means they received it harshly, read between the lines and inferred things that weren't necessarily there. Nevertheless, I was quiet and listened to her as she explained.

"I have a 2-year-old daughter who goes to a really good Christian day care. My husband and I both work, but it isn't as if we are doing this to deliberately lead my child to aggressive behavior. My daughter is a good kid, and that article just slams on moms who are trying the best they can to support their family."

She grew angrier as she spoke. She continued, "Focus on the Family is a ministry that is supposed to be reaching out to young couples, but the truth is that many of them have no choice but to work. I can say this for sure: *I have no choice* but to have my child in day care, and *I am trying* to do the best I can."

She went on to tell me more about of her specific situation: Her husband was a banker making a less-than-mediocre income. She and her husband were still paying off student loans from private colleges. They came to Colorado Springs on a leap of faith, but the move racked up a credit card bill they also had to pay off. "I have no choice," she repeated.

Her situation was not unique. Focus on the Family had nearly 1,500 employees at the time, and there were lots of working mothers among them. Almost paradoxically, we published articles about the harms of two-parent incomes and the accompanying problems of debt and day care. I felt like I was an anomaly—one of the only dads in the ministry who worked a job *and* ran a home business to make ends meet and to allow my wife to take care of our children at home.

"I admit, it is not easy," I said to the working mom in my cubicle. "I, too, work my tail off to provide for my nine children."

Her jaw dropped. She clearly didn't know me as well as she had thought. "Nine children? You have *nine children*? How do you do it?"

I was glad she asked, and the conversation led to several ideas that might help her alleviate her financial burden. Like so many things in life, she was bogged down with an incorrect perspective, a point of view that kept her options limited. She and her husband ran after dual incomes, dual careers, dual educations with the dream of having the "perfect" marriage and raising the "perfect" family.

So why did having children—necessary to *create* that perfect family—seem to complicate her dream?

Life is complicated, but children aren't. Children just want a mom and dad to love them and raise them. Our fast-paced world convinces young couples to build wealth and material possessions. Even in Christian environments like Focus on the Family, the idea of what makes a good family is very different from what a child would conceive. Really, what child prefers day care over his or her mother?

Which brings us back to loving another child. Because one of the most popular hesitations parents have to doing so is *"We can't afford it!"* Debt, mortgage, work and the lack of *stuff* weigh on families. Children cost thousands of dollars just to be born, and the bills stack up thereafter. If you listen to modern financial experts, they pull crazy numbers out of the air that claim the total cost of having a child—considering all expenses from birth to college graduation—is hundreds of thousands of dollars.

We very much understand living on a limited income. Wendy and I married in 1992, and we become an instant family of four when I adopted Alicia and Alissa. We lived in a two-bedroom apartment and, like the mother I spoke with at Focus on the Family, resorted to day care. Wendy worked full time as a customer service representative while I worked early morning shifts in a produce department before heading to school every day to finish my degree. Our first baby together came before I graduated, and so we, too, sought out a Christian day care—that of a dear family we knew in our church—to keep up with our family goals.

I eventually graduated, and the day Wendy quit her job was a day to celebrate. But I didn't get a teaching job right away, and for two years was on call for 28 school districts in central Minnesota as a substitute teacher. And then my first regular teaching job was nothing to be giddy about: The base salary started at just $16,900. So I took the job and worked two extra classes, along with becoming a debate coach and serving as the school photographer. In the summers I would roof houses with a friend from church (making more—no kidding—than I did as a teacher). We were diligent to spend money within our means, avoiding consumer debt at all costs. And by doing so we managed to scrounge just enough money ($7,000 at the time) to make a down payment on our first home.

These were financially tough times, but we were young and in love, able to take on the challenges that came our way. So the idea that parents "have no choice" seems doubtful to us. Difficult, sure, but *impossible?* We never settled with this premise. Financially speaking, we've turned doubt on its head. Children *are* blessings, and being poor doesn't turn them into curses.

When we were featured on *Kids by the Dozen*, the most popular question from parents who saw the show was how we "afforded" so many children. On our website, we conducted a poll, and the results showed overwhelmingly that—even though it wasn't the theme of the show—finances were what people thought was most interesting. Our second-most popular FAQ was, and still is, "How do you keep your monthly grocery bill below $700 per month?"

The world is going through an economic recession. Headlines riddle the news with statements about how difficult the economy is. And the economy is reflective of how much revenue people have, which isn't as much as it used to be, it seems. What people can purchase with their money is shrinking as inflation is hitting the costs of common items in the stores. Just look at staples such as milk, eggs and rice. Where we live, their prices have seen double-digit increases in the past few years.

All bad news. Does this challenge our faith that God provides? It sure does. But with the challenge comes the opportunity to let God enter your family life and take care of you. He has done so time and time again for our family, and He will for you. Much of it has to do with a simple change of heart, an attitude that is above finances and in the atmosphere of faith.

Creativity Is Next to Godliness

Financial problems often emerge when families refuse to adjust to economic changes. Well aware of this pitfall, we're constantly adjusting our eating habits according to what things cost where we live. Adaptability is creativity, an "image of God" trait. We are created in the image of God, and we believe creativity is what God expects from us. So financially tough times bring out the best in us.

When we respond to economic pressures that squeeze our lifestyle, God smiles on our efforts to adapt to those pressures. Rich, poor or somewhere in between, every family must endure financially difficult times. In fact, understanding this reality and embracing the challenges that come our way is better learned early in marriage.

Especially when the pregnancy test comes back positive. It may surprise you—maybe even shock you. But it will not cripple you. Change, especially the change that a child brings, is very good. Every child is a blessing from God largely because the child prods us to grow up and stay grown up. We aren't able to excuse immaturity or slothfulness when a child comes along.

In every area of our life we have learned to adapt to the challenges that hit our family. Even through the short span when Wendy worked outside the home so that I could finish up school, we didn't fool ourselves into thinking we "had no choice." We adapted to our circumstances, made it work for a time, then moved on to a better family arrangement. Every mom and dad has this ability.

Take something as simple as cooking for your family. Working mothers often feed their families prepackaged meals. You save a tremendous amount of money when you cook your own meals. We're in the habit of planning out what is for dinner by 10 a.m. We have it out of the freezer thawing or in the Crock-Pot stewing. We are able to take advantage of the ingredients that we have on hand rather than serve meals that cost more because so much of the price is pegged to marketing and packaging. And beyond the fact that homemade meals cost less, they're also much healthier!

Compared to the dual-income family with one child, we likely spend $10 less every evening on dinner. Voila: $3,650 savings per year. That's a big chunk off the grocery budget.

Keeping up with the latest styles and trends can also place an unneeded financial burden on your family. When kids grow out of their clothes, who thinks, "Whom can we pass these clothes on to because we don't want to throw them away?" Yep. It's the Jeubs! One of our kids is bound to fit into them. And when we're completely finished, we pass the clothes on to another family. There is no shame in that, and never mind the cultural expectation to have your children wear all new clothes. Truthfully, we'd go broke if we followed this expectation of buying new clothes for each of our children. We don't do this, and we don't believe any family must.

We also refuse to waste money on name-brand items. We rarely buy anything other than store generics because there are rarely any differences in the products. We have a friend who opened up a retail food store. She told us about touring a potato chip factory where the assembly machine loaded up bags of brand-labeled potato chips. Then the conveyor changed paths and the bags were replaced with a store-named generic label. Same exact potato chips, different bags.

We rarely buy in anything but bulk, too. And this is an inherent *advantage* to being a big family. In the world of large-family grocery shopping, bigger is better—and it's certainly more efficient. We buy 300 pounds of oatmeal every year from a local co-op, for instance. It lasts 12-18 months in sealed containers as we gradually use it for breakfasts, pie crusts, cookies and all sorts of other baking recipes. Compared to the tiny 24 ounce Quaker box, we're practically stealing the oatmeal.

Stores will drop prices significantly when the expiration date on the label becomes a past date instead of a future date. Truth be told, we rarely buy bread that's "fresh." We frequent a bread outlet and fill our 15-cubic-foot chest freezer with loaves of Oroweat. This day-old bread is the same price as the flimsy, cheap bread we find at the supermarket, but is twice the consistency and much heartier for our children.

A side note: We don't bake our own bread. Though many do and enjoy it, through the 1990s there was a cultural expectation among stay-at-home mothers to bake their own bread. We looked into it and eventually concluded that a few hundred dollars worth of hardware and ingredients would end up costing more than the loaves we liked from the bread outlet. Add to that the labor of messing up the kitchen and the cost of running the oven all day long for a family our size, and we're glad we blew off this expectation. For us, it was a no-brainer: *No way* are we baking our own bread!

Subsequently, we've had mothers at conferences come to us as if we've lifted the world from their shoulders. "Thank you, thank you,"

Love Another Child

they say, "for telling me you don't bake your own bread! I'm never baking my own bread again!"

We don't clip coupons, either, by the way. And we get the same response from mothers who were told they should play the coupon game. We considered all the time it took to comb through coupons and compared it to the savings, and our decision to axe the project was an easy one. Make no mistake about it: Coupons are meant to get you to buy certain products, not to save you money. There isn't anything inherently evil about coupons, but they do control the buyer, not the other way around.

One of our least visited aisles in the grocery store is the cereal aisle. Most families eat cereal and milk for breakfast every morning as if families for generations have eaten boxed, sugar-coated air. We hardly ever have this kind of cereal in our home. Instead, our children eat bagels and cream cheese, oatmeal, eggs and sausage, fruit (an abundance of whatever is in season at the time). Not only are we getting better food, but we're spending a lot less money, all because we're not fooled into eating what the marketers tell us to eat.

I (Wendy) don't buy cleaning supplies at the supermarket. I buy a $1 gallon of ammonia, put 1/16 of it into a spray bottle along with water. It becomes a cleaner for everything in the house. I use Dawn Dish Detergent, diluted with water, as a stronger spot cleaner. These two solutions cost less than $3, and they substitute for cleaning supplies valued at 10 times the amount. Like cereal, the cleaning supply aisle in the supermarket is one of the flashiest in the store, but it's one we hardly ever shop in.

There are all sorts of cultural expectations put out there by marketers that end up costing tons of money. A biggie is soft drinks, and so we rarely buy canned or bottled soda. We drink a lot of water, fresh from our Colorado well, which is probably cleaner than store-bought bottled water. Our favorite drink is Kombucha, a healthy tea that we brew ourselves. The drink costs $2.49 for a 20-ounce bottle at any health food store, but we brew it by the gallon at home. (My first cookbook has a complete explanation for distilling and brewing Kombucha.)

31

We make a habit of watering down our orange juice when we make a can of concentrated. Come to think of it, we stretch a lot of our food. Common meat substitutes such as rice, oatmeal and beans are regulars in our cooking. We mix pork in with our game meat (which Chris hunts himself). We beat eggs and crackers into our hamburger. What are we missing? Absolutely nothing. We have a loving and well-fed family, the bills are paid and life goes on. Why wouldn't we welcome another child into this?

Poverty and Provision

Finances—not necessarily the lack of finances—cause stress in families. Matters of money trigger huge rifts in marriages. But with faith, adaptability and wisdom, your financial life does not need to be so worrisome.

There is a realistic caution that all families need to own. The Bible talks directly to parents: "If anyone does not provide for his relatives, and especially for his immediate family, he has denied the faith and is worse than an unbeliever" (1 Timothy 5:8). Heavy. The responsibility for parents to provide for their family is a must. There is no compromise in this area of our family life. But should parents restrict having children if that provision seems to be threatened? You'll have a difficult time finding a verse to justify that position. Nowhere in Scripture are children seen as burdens. Children are reinforced as blessings throughout.

So what are parents to do? Times are tough, and having another child appears to be irresponsible. At the very least it seems that loving another child would mean loving the one (or ones) you have a little less. You know, you're going to have to do a lot of praying about that perspective. Personally, we have never had that conviction on our hearts, and we have not found scriptural precedent to support such an idea. While God opens and closes the womb (Genesis 29:31), many people, independently from God, choose to do so.

What we can stand confidently and say is this: *Poverty does not deter happiness.* We've lived underneath the poverty line for most of our married life. In fact, if you count all our children, we are very close to what the government calls "extreme" poverty. However, our lives couldn't be more fruitful! There is nothing that holds us back from opportunity, fellowship and a fantastic family. We are very happy people who have more than we could have hoped for. The poverty rubric seems to indicate that we need to be depressed or walk around sad, saying, "Woe are us! We're extremely impoverished." Nonsense. In our lives, in our hearts, in our children—there is joy and happiness. If anyone tries to tell you that you shouldn't be happy because you're financially strapped, blow them off. It's a lie, plain and simple. Poverty and wealth have nothing to do with happiness at all.

Financial problems are a given; for most of us, they will always be there. Parents shouldn't make their poverty (or fear of poverty) inhibitors to the blessings that can come from God. This was the same crummy attitude Jesus' disciples gave Him when they complained over the woman pouring expensive perfume over His head and feet. "Why are you bothering this woman? She has done a beautiful thing to me," He responded. "The poor you will always have with you, but you will not always have me" (Matthew 26:10-11). Likewise, when we fret over finances at the expense of our relationship with Jesus Christ, we fret in vain.

Anxiety over finances—common as it may be—reflects a lack of understanding more than it does reality. Are we really surprised at how much economic ignorance exists among couples? From an early age, a dysfunctional view of economics was drilled into most of us. We were taught to think finances are finite, that getting a job is the highest calling in life, and that conformity is a virtue. We were also taught *not* to innovate, *not* to shake the boat, to avoid creation. It's the pedagogy of the 20th century, of which we're products.

Ask people what makes the economy tick, and you'll get an assortment of answers: money, gold, the DOW or NASDAQ indexes, and so on. Few people understand that the backbone of an economy is *people*. Human beings. The ingenuity of the human mind is priceless, and each and every one's contribution to society is what builds the economy. What everyone else points to are merely tangible measurements we use to rate the effectiveness of the amount of creativity in the economy.

Take, for instance, money. A paper dollar is really just a piece of paper that costs six or seven cents to print but is actually worth perhaps only half a cent. The dollar is assigned value—understood by every person in our society. *People* give the dollar weight. Same thing with gold. What, really, is gold, after all? It's not much different than lead, just a bit prettier. The value people put on gold is what gives it worth. It is all about people, their collective perceptions, and what they—together—choose to perceive.

So what if we live in a 2,400-square-foot house and we bring home a fraction of what most families bring home. Are we impoverished? Hardly. We have 16 human beings we're raising that will all contribute to a greater social economy. There is freedom in this perspective, one that keeps us free from financial worry and open to more of the same blessings that each one of our children has given us.

Toughen up, parents! Be the optimists that your children want you to be. We cannot emphasize enough the importance of changing your attitude toward money. Too many families cling to a dysfunctional relationship with money, perhaps loving money rather than God's calling in their lives. Wherever this perspective came from, parents should kick it straight out of the field of their lives forever.

The Steward of Your Heritage

Your family heritage will be defined by your children's perception of you. It has little to do with with how many toys you spoil them, and everything to do with how you utilize the gifts God gives you. Whatever resources are at your disposal, let the creative juices flow; take them on with unyielding enthusiasm.

I (Wendy) keep a price list and a calculator in my purse, incredibly handy in a rapidly fluctuating economy. I write down the name of the store, how much I paid for a particular item, and then compare the prices to previous weeks. This habit keeps me on top of what the deals are and gives me an understanding of what is *actually* a good deal and what is merely marketing hype.

You know you are susceptible to grocery store marketing when you stand in your pantry and see food that has stacked up over the weeks and months, much of which you will not use anyway. These are often coupon-promoted items that seemed like great deals at the time but are nothing more than waste if you don't eat them. A good steward keeps her wits about her when shopping, only buying food she would normally use. The supermarkets have their "blowout" items every week—but don't buy them just because they're on sale. Instead, buy them because you will use them. This is how you should read the weekly flyer when you shop. Don't look for the good deals; look for the good deals on things you normally use. Stock up on them and you'll be truly spending your money wisely.

Do your best to stick to that shopping list. I will take 10 meals that I want to have in the coming week, make my list, and "shop" in my own pantry and freezer first. Many of the goods I need for the week are already there. The poor steward will think, "I'm hungry, so I'm going to go to the store and figure out what's for dinner." But studies show that such a shopping lifestyle will increase your grocery spending by 30 percent. The stores end up telling you what to buy and what to eat rather than the food you already have on hand. That's shopping with your gut rather than your brain.

A good steward will become a student of the local deals. We used to not know what the egg cartons meant by "Grade A." Was there a "Grade B"? Apparently so. When supermarkets handle eggs more often—as when they are transferred from one carton to another if a neighboring egg happens to break—the stores mark them down significantly. Same eggs, lower grade. But here's the trick: Our local grocery store hardly ever puts those eggs out on the floor. So when we found this out, we began asking the dairy guy for the Grade B eggs. We saved a ton.

In some ways, being a student of the deals involves looking at the bigger picture—or the yearly cycle, which often revolves around holidays. Every Thanksgiving, our local supermarkets mark down turkeys to $5 or $6—when they are regularly over $30. So we buy at least a half-dozen extra turkeys right before Thanksgiving. At Christmas and Easter, you can find cheaper ham, and eggs sometimes dip to half their regular cost.

But being a good steward doesn't always mean *spending* less; it sometimes means *using* less. A habit we make when grocery shopping is looking at the weight first rather than the price. Bacon, for example, is packaged for those who look at price rather than weight. A 12-ounce pack of bacon looks exactly the same as a 16-ounce pack of bacon, but it's priced lower. Most people have cell phones with calculators, so use it to figure out how to get the most for your money. We don't go into the store looking for the cheapest stuff; we go in thinking about how to get the biggest bang for our buck.

I have published two cookbooks and am collecting recipes for a third. And threaded through all my recipes is this reality: *We eat like kings.* Being frugal does not equate with being cheap. *Cheap* carries the connotation of lower value, as if we are sacrificing quality in order to save a few cents. Frugality doesn't condone sacrifice; it means getting the most for your money, which is a principle of good stewardship. Our family eats very well, and our choices at the grocery store are testimony to this fact.

We did "once-a-month cooking" for seven years straight when we had a family about half the size of the one we have now. Back then, we cooked 30 meals on a budget of $100. Today, that would be tough, but we know families who are even more frugal than us. And we still live by some of the once-a-month cooking principles: we super-size some of the meals, then drop the extra food in the freezer for a later day. Ultimately, this saves money because it keeps you out of the store where you inevitably spend more money.

Whatever God has blessed you with, get creative and figure out ways to double it or even triple it. Don't grumble about it like the Israelites did when they were given manna. They should have gotten creative and made manna waffles and manna soufflé, like the late Christian singer Keith Green said. When Chris shoots an elk or a deer, we put it to use, every bit of it. When we lived in Minnesota and had a strong harvest of tomatoes or corn, we put it up. When certain produce items are plentiful at the store or farmer's market, we buy them and put them to use. Whatever is at our disposal, we use.

Do you know that this is a principle of economics that entrepreneurs live by? Millionaires have been known to be some of the most frugal people on the planet, always looking for opportunity to get the best bang for their buck (or their million bucks). To the wealthy, an idle dollar is a wasted dollar. Yet in today's consumer-centered society, parents have come to think very narrowly about the dollars they've been blessed with.

Most of us know the parable of the talents, the story Jesus told of the three servants given responsibility for a certain amount of money. The first two were good stewards who doubled their money with investments and creative thinking. The third servant buried his money out of fear. "You wicked, lazy servant!" was the king's response, stripping him of his one coin and giving it to the one with the most.

It isn't poverty that's a shame. It's an impoverished *mentality*. What a shame it is when parents carry this weight around their neck. Rather than putting their resources to work and together fending for themselves, they bury their God-given talents and accept the impoverished mentality. And that's a serious shame.

We've met people who boil with anger at our message of frugality, largely because they assume we're living on government assistance of some sort. But we don't receive a dime of government subsidy. We could easily qualify, but we don't bother. We could fill our cupboards with food from food stamps, the food shelf, WIC, you name it. Our heat could be paid for and our mortgage written off. We would easily qualify for medical assistance, but we haven't since my single-parenting days. The angry folks who think *they're* paying for our household items through taxation, we quiet with the truth.

Parents too quickly give up as a result of financial stress and give in to dependency. We encourage you to fight that temptation at all costs. It is much easier today than ever before to seek aid to supplement your lifestyle, but doing so fuels the impoverished mentality; frugal creativity banishes it. In a local newspaper, we were compared to families who complained about their need to earn welfare equivalent to a working wage. "How do [the Jeubs] do it? They're smart, disciplined and resourceful," the article proclaimed. "They derive happiness from love, not gluttony and excess. ... An American family of seven that struggles on $76,000 a year is spoiled rotten."[4]

Don't misread our frugal message as judgment against those who do accept government assistance. Rather, for those who are at that place in their life, at least read what government assistance says it is: *assistance.* Do all you can to get off of it. If it helps even more, call it what it really is: an ugly political trap that enslaves you to a system that cares nothing for you or your family. Welfare is a vicious cycle that keeps your family from a godly heritage that is much greater than a government bureaucrat can promise.

These are tough times, we know, but nothing is impossible for the family that dedicates itself to the plan God has in mind. This attitude is the attitude of the good steward, the one whom God wants to bless with abundance. Abundance in what? It may not be money. It may be children, good neighbors or friends, or several other things that many wealthy people do not have. Set both aside from one another—a healthy bank account balance and healthy family relationships—and choose. We choose relationships, and we do what we must with our tight finances.

Don't look down on frugality. Such snobbery takes for granted God-given ingenuity and resourcefulness. Too many couples choose barrenness to afford material possessions, fearing poverty as if the need to be frugal is a deadly disease. We've known people who look down on us from their 10,000-square-foot homes and incomes 10 times ours, yet they have no children. We do not envy them. Who cares if they look down their noses at us? We have more love, more heritage, more fruitfulness than all their 401(k)'s, pension plans and hoarded savings combined.

Every time our budget shrinks, we respond with renewed enthusiasm. Virtually every family has had to have those uncomfortable meetings with the kids, the kind that explain that finances are tough and some sacrifices have to be made. Next time you need to do that, turn the discussion around to a positive. "God wants us to be creative, kids, so let's figure something out!"

This encourages your children to be resourceful and helpful. And believe it or not they'll actually *love* doing it. The harm doesn't come from tightening your belts a little, it comes from leaving our children with the false impression that they are merely consumers of the family's resources. When they venture off into adulthood, they will not be a blessing to the people around them if they don't learn how to be a blessing in their own family. Frugal families are constantly trying to think of ways to use less and be less of a burden to each other. This is healthy thinking.

We turn our water heater down to its "vacation" setting every night, for example, skipping a cycle or two of keeping water hot while we sleep. We make a habit of it, the same as locking the front door. We turn down the house's heater, too, in winter months. There is no reason to cycle the water heater or run the regular heater when you're snuggled up in bed already. We also pool our resources with other families, forming cooperatives. We accept secondhand clothes from churches and individuals, and we form clothing exchanges. Our creative ideas flow from our frugality.

Here is a key principle of frugality, which is also a principle of business: return on investment (ROI). What you spend should always give you more value in return. Cheaper is not always better, and because of that we buy nice dog food for our pets. Why? Because they will eat less, their coats will be shinier and they will be healthier. So there's a robust return on the money spent. We buy some brand names when there's a compelling reason to do so. Some brand name paper towels, for instance, are perforated at the half-sheet, so you use fewer of them when cleaning up spills. Off-brand paper towels may be cheaper, but we inevitably end up using more.

Creativity—the "image of God" trait—looks at finances in a whole different light. Rather than conforming to marketing trends and cultural expectations, we continue to grow our family and transform our perspective in everything we do. Financially speaking, we are as fulfilled as we can be. Our wealth has more to do with how we perceive our wellbeing than it does with the amount of money we have in the bank.

There is a sharp contrast between the creative and the consumer. The consumer believes poverty brings anxiety; the creative believes poverty brings opportunity. The consumer seeks cheap; the creative seeks efficiency. The consumer values money; the creative values return on investment. The consumer will often feel ripped off; the creative feels good when paying a fair price. The consumer feels guilty when spending; the creative enjoys the riches of life. The consumer often envies the rich; the creative believes everyone can be rich. The consumer typically appeals to the government for bailouts or aid; the creative seeks God for answers and solutions.

And here's the kicker: Consumers always have financial problems. It doesn't matter if they're rich or poor. They consume; that's who they are. So their consumption will never be enough to satisfy. We know miserable wealthy people, and we don't want that misery for our family. The creative always has financial freedom, and it doesn't matter if you are rich or poor.

The secret to wealth and prosperity has nothing to do with a finite amount of money. True economists know this. Prosperity has everything to do with human ingenuity. Human beings, their creative minds, their adaptability and utilization of the gifts God has dropped into their laps is what a life is built upon. This is building a heritage.

And this is what the Jeub family has made: a life of brothers and sisters walking with God. This is the richest of lives.

A Lesson in Hunting

Environment is another one of those loaded terms; it means different things to different people. To us, it is our surroundings, the life we make together, our shelter and our livelihood. The 1 Timothy 5:8 verse about provision is about a family's environment, and it includes more than simply financial provision. Our children are taught the valuable lessons of good stewardship (a lesson that is easier taught in poor families than rich), along with honor and respect for each other—to the *environment* around them.

There isn't a better example, in our opinion, than hunting. We claim that we "hunt for food," but that really is with our tongues firmly planted in our cheeks. After what we spend on traveling, ammo, gear, etc., hunting is a very expensive method for gathering meat. We hunt for much deeper, more eternal reasons than meat. These include heritage, conservation, family and rich moments in God's great outdoors. Sure, there is something to be said for taking advantage of the sport and getting as much in return as possible. From the permits we buy to the land we scout, our minds are on maximizing our hunting potential. (We're *always* focused on ROI.)

The Jeubs are hunters, but we aren't rowdy, and we don't shoot our guns in the air! We are conservationists who believe hunting is a heritage, much like farming. We even call our game "harvest." Hunting falls into that category of land and wildlife management that is necessary for a healthy environment. This is good stewardship of the earth, a biblical mandate. After dropping our game, we make a habit of taking off our hats, kneeling and laying a hand on the warm animal to give thanks to God for the provision He's blessed us with.

We choose hunting as a family activity largely because of the valuable life lessons it teaches: conservation, diligence, nature skills, camaraderie, safety and survival. But at the top of the list is *provision*. The children are eager to contribute to the provision of our family. They know that their hard work and diligent hunt brings food to the table. This realization sinks deep into their souls. The kids become creators of provision, walking in the image of God.

Most hunters have a meat market process their animals, but we butcher our own. It gives the entire family a piece of the action, even the little kids not yet old enough to go out on the hunt. A traditional practice after wrapping the steaks and roasts is marking the name of the hunter on the package. Reading "Lydia's Tenderloin Steaks" when the meat is pulled from the freezer four months later is quite a rush for the child responsible. What better confidence builder is there than sharing a hearty elk steak meal with 16 others—who are all saying, "This elk tastes great!"—knowing that *you* were the one to provide.

All parents are called to provide for their family. We may brew up all sorts of impoverished, desperate situations in our minds before each baby comes, wondering how we could possibly survive. But then, when the child arrives, we make it all work out. We stop asking "how" and we just do it. In fact, we find that providing for our family is a great life full of purpose and pride.

We've been having child after child for the past two decades, and that thrill of harvest never gets old, nor does it ever come close to being impossible. We make our finances work out, and so will you.

---

4 - Our Environment

"The battle to feed humanity is over. In the 1970s, the world will undergo famines. Hundreds of millions of people are going to starve to death in spite of any crash programs embarked upon now. Population control is the only answer." —Paul Ehrlich, in his 1968 bestseller "The Population Bomb"

Here's our proposition to young couples: You *can* have and love another child. We don't think we're proposing the preposterous. We sometimes wonder how this perspective got lost. We're merely reinforcing something many young couples already have on their minds. Doesn't every couple ask themselves about procreation, bearing children and extending their heritage? In quiet moments, alone, we sure hope so. A life that doesn't consider this is a shallow life, a self-centered one. Married couples should have such intimate discussions. The bond of love between man and woman naturally begs the question, "Could we have a child?" And for the family with one or two, "Could we love another?"

Let's face it, though, the normal conversation goes the opposite direction. Does jumping on the birth control bandwagon make anybody bat an eye nowadays? Avoiding children throughout a couple's productive years has been the mantra since the 1960s. Encouragement to have children—the message of the Jeub family— is out of the ordinary. It takes explanation, a flat-out rebuttal to an underlying expectation of our modern day. The expectation is to pursue a litany of ambitions—children and a family low on the list.

Career, travel, education, sports—even romantic relationships can (how ironic!) get in the way of a couple's ambition to have and love children.

There is an underpinning to this cultural norm that's quite sinister. There is no loud cry, "Children curse the earth! Don't have children!" Instead, the message is subtle, more difficult to recognize when you hear it. The arguments are comforting to young couples in that they encourage us to hold on to our youth and walk through our reproductive years "free" from the confines of family life. The years go by faster than the 20-something realizes, though, and they soon stand in the middle of their middle-age, alone, barren and wondering what it would be like to have had children of their own.

Children. They're blessings. Always. That's the truth right before our eyes. We voluntarily disguise them as something else. As money magnets and as environment killers, crowding an already crowded planet. Two's company and three's a crowd, right? Besides, what would my parents/neighbors/siblings/co-workers think about us being pregnant *again*? Another child will bring back diapers, sleepless nights, having to figure out day care. They scream and mess up the house and rearrange my nice, neat, controlled life. On and on the litany goes.

But this litany reveals a reality about the parents, not the child. These views are selfish, and that's a sad way to view children. Sure, there are times of exhaustion and anxiety, but that's more than acceptable when considering the heritage that comes with the work. Children—your children—are a huge advantage to you personally and is a significant asset to the planet. One person *can* make a world of difference.

Here's the doozy that couples embrace: *Children are a detriment to our environment.* They may not come right out and say it this way, but it's what they believe. In their minds, they imagine another child exhausting their family, just "another mouth to feed," a liability to society as a whole. These couples believe that restricting the birth of another child is actually doing themselves—and society—a favor.

This kind of thinking dominates discussions between husbands and wives. "Planning" parenting is more about *avoiding* children than it is about having them. And no doubt the founder of Planned Parenthood, Margaret Sanger, whose eugenically inspired agenda included weeding out inferior races, would be pleased. Today Planned Parenthood is the leading provider of abortions, and they have been caught numerous times covering for statutory rape,[5] aiding sexual promiscuity[6] in underage children and advocating for hideous procedures such as partial birth abortion.[7]

Volumes of research have exposed the mantra of such "family planning," wherein practices include infanticide, abortion and forced sterilization. It's a hideous history, one that we believe will someday be looked back upon with great sadness and humiliation.

The history of loving another child, on the other hand, is rich and rewarding. The blessings of children have always been as natural as the rising sun. And it's only in the past 50-100 years that this "grand" social experiment of "planned parenthood" has interrupted them. Let's cry for China's one-child policy (which actually means aborting all children that follow, in a way that painfully recalls— and weirdly twists—Pharaoh's ancient-Egypt attempt to control the growth of the Israelites). But it's the West that has more of a problem with *voluntarily* limiting children. Aborting children, staying on the pill for decades, holding onto youth for as long as possible—these are dysfunctional choices that are now ruling relationships. We walk through our lives thinking we're on the right track, but really we're posing, avoiding the great blessings that children bring to our lives and to the world.

Abortion is made all the more awful when it defines a personal *choice*. You often hear statistics about the number of aborted babies in the U.S. since the 1973 Roe v. Wade decision forced states to legalize abortion. But here's a less often cited fact: Millions of women have *voluntarily killed their unborn children*. That's *heavy*. Admitting to this is a huge, emotional feat. These young girls, led by the hand by a kind lady wearing white, live with this reality for the rest of their lives.

Admission to simple wrongdoing is fairly easy. "Whoops, my bad!" doesn't take heavenly conviction. Admission to *believing* something *untrue* is like moving a mountain. Millions of well-meaning people support the work of Planned Parenthood, so defining it as *immoral* is difficult to do—and accept. It's humiliating at the very least. But the evidence keeps coming. The deeper the person falls into the lie, the deeper their heels dig, the harder it is to come to the truth.

And believing lies never bears fruit in our lives. We make a serious mistake when we follow preconceived notions that are based on false premises. So many of us are walking posers, often recognizable to anyone but ourselves. Do you know people in relationships that are going nowhere, yet they insist they're in love? Ever had a job that was pointless, with a jerk for a boss, but for a time you thought you had a future there? A tough breakup or a firing perhaps knocked you back into reality. And you now refer back to these hardships as "blessings in disguise." At the time, though, you were too blind to see the truth right before your eyes.

Obviously, our family has rejected "family planning," and we're personally grateful for the clarity that decision has brought. We swim against the current, and we're proud of that. Such a life is remarkable and fruitful. It took a good deal of meditation and prayer to overcome popular opinion, as we're sure it does for most couples. When couples are honest about the truth—when they're walking with God and genuinely open to what He has in store for them—it doesn't take too much to convince them to love another child. These couples discover freedom in family, a liberation from the Planned Parenthood lie that kept true joy from them.

Our lives serve as testimony that, contrary to the populist argument, having more than the expected number of children brings a great deal of blessing to a family. This may prompt horrified gasps at a Planned Parenthood conference, but it resolutely relieves parents of the burden they carry. You see, the agenda to limit childbearing is largely based on faulty premises, some of them complete bunk. They have been proven time and again to be flatly wrong, yet they continue to be explained as if they've never been disproved. Many parents, unfortunately, hold onto these ideas. With a little bit of thought, parents who are honest with themselves and with God can accept with confidence that loving another child will not bring the drastic consequences that we have been taught to believe.

The Earth Is Not Overpopulated

We are amazed at how many still hold onto the outdated notion that the world is overpopulated. The cry from the wilderness has been coming from academia for decades, like Chicken Little crying, "The sky is falling!" According to progressive thought, we're at the tipping point where the world's resources are not sustainable for an increasing population. Trouble is, this tipping point has been falsely predicted for the past half-century. In 1968, Paul Ehrlich predicted all sorts of catastrophes in his book *The Population Bomb:*

- That famines would cripple the world in the 1970s and 1980s.
- That natural resources would be depleted from the world's demanding population.
- That hundreds of millions of people would starve to death.
- That food riots would force world governments to take drastic measures to reduce population.
- That by 1985 ramifications of overpopulation would cause enough death to drop "the earth's population to some acceptable level, like 1.5 billion people."[8]

When Ehrlich wrote this, the global population stood at 3.5 billion. As of October 2010, the world's occupancy rate has doubled, sitting at just one tick below 7 billion. And none of these catastrophes have come close to occurring. What should reasonable and scientifically mature people do with such modern "prophets"? Well, perhaps not what we actually *do* do with them, because Ehrlich is currently a tenured professor at Stanford, having been showered with honorary degrees and awards. He's a frequent lecturer at universities around the world, heralded by some as a great environmentalist. Shouldn't they (and he) be embarrassed? For an analysis of his predictions show them to be utter nonsense. Yet the beating drum of progressives keeps pounding out this message: a rising population is bringing doom to the planet.

He's wrong. They're wrong. And sympathy for their assumptions is an even greater wrong. Because granting this premise allows the limiting of children—sometimes through horrific means. The next time someone tries to tell you that the world is overpopulated, push back by saying, "The world needs *more* people." When their jaws drop to the ground, take the opportunity to give them a sobering drink of cool logic.

The picture of an overpopulated earth is prejudiced, a picture in the mind that some fearmonger placed there. Watch any news broadcast or documentary on population, and they inevitably show shots of downtown Shanghai or starving masses in Calcutta. The logical leap is tied to these highly emotional pictures. "It is because the world is overpopulated that these people are harmed," they say. But it's an illusion. Only the pictures make it look like the claim is true. For once we'd like to see pictures of the vast and beautiful plains of Wyoming when a news anchor announces a spike in world population.

We believe there is a natural break in perspective in just how big the earth really is. The world is vast, bigger than our little minds can truly fathom. We take the opportunity to show this to our children when we go elk hunting. Elk are huge creatures, four times the size of deer. When we harvest a cow or bull, we literally have to start the butchering process in the field to get the animal to our camp. There are half-a-million elk in Colorado, and we Jeubs venture out every year to attempt to fill our freezer with the best (organic) meat a person can eat.

Our imaginations run wild in anticipation of the hunt. We watch movies that show trophy bulls at every forest turn. But these images, like the images of starving children in India, give a false impression. They make us think that the elk are all over the place, that we merely need to set up our lawn chairs and wait for them to walk into our crosshairs. Hunters who think such things are always disappointed. We have often hunted for days at a time without seeing a single elk. And when we do see some, perhaps from a distance, and run to find them, these 800-pound beasts seem to utterly vanish in the vast wilderness. We call elk "ghosts of the forest," for these huge animals have an uncanny ability to disappear at the drop of a hat.

The lesson is simple: The world is a vast place. It takes a tremendous amount of gullibility to think it small and crowded. A total of 400,000 hunters enter the mountains of Colorado every year, and 80 percent of them go home with nothing. The earth is not a tiny place. If it was as tiny as the population alarmists say, you'd think at least guys with high-powered rifles would be a little more successful. But it just isn't so. Contrary to what our little minds can fathom, this is *not* a small world after all. And it has plenty of hiding places for humans and elk alike. To continue thinking otherwise, you'll need to go live in another world.

It comes as no surprise that population control proponents live in large cities in little apartments close to their work cubicles in skyscrapers. No wonder they feel cramped. Their thinking is ruled by Hollywood horror that appeals to flailing fears. They err to think that human beings—in fact, their very existence—is bringing the earth to a tipping point any day now. And they err even more when they determine that "because" the world must be overpopulated, they must advocate and even legislate population control. They need to go hunting, maybe drive through Nebraska on the way. Perhaps they'd come to realize that the world has a whole lot of elbowroom.

World Resources Are Not Depleting

The high-rise residents who think everyone lives the way they do will cling to economic fallacies to justify their opinion. People need resources, they argue, and there are limited resources to provide for a growing population. Again, don't give them the satisfaction of conceding the premise. This world is full of resources, and it is a false claim to say the world's population cannot be sustained.

Think of the consequences of so-called overpopulation: famine, starvation, mob riots, and so on. Ask yourself, *Where are these places? Can these places not provide enough food for their people?* Sometimes you'll hear of mass starvations in arid climates cut off from supply routes. But more often news headlines of these sorts come from agriculturally rich countries such as China, India and Central Africa. Resources are plentiful in these areas. Why, then, is starvation a problem? It isn't because of the resources, and it isn't because of population numbers. It has everything to do with economics—and how they're run.

India serves as a great example of how economic socialist theories crippled the globe's second-most populous country. For four decades following the 1947 liberation of India, socialist party leaders ruled unchecked. Poverty and famine reigned, and social engineers erroneously pointed to the population surge as the problem. Then the economic tide began to turn in 1990, gradually freeing the country from the shackles of socialist policies. Today, India's population is much larger than in 1990, yet India leads the world in economic growth and prosperity.

The same goes for China. For most of us growing up, the dinnertime mantra was, Eat your food because there were starving children in China! And there were. But not because of the population of the country. China was more Communist than Russia through the Cold War, but, like India, its leaders slowly started to release their grip on the economic throttle in the 1990s. Today, China is one of the fastest developing economies on the planet. While the political culture is still Communist, free market principles have energized the landscape. (The one-child policy will devastate the country in the next 20 years, but that's another story.)

Consider any area of the world where population is thought to be the problem. Inevitably, it is always in the grip of a socialistic dictatorship. The elite are fat; the masses are starving. This has nothing to do with depleted resources and everything to do with the economic system that distributes them.

These People Should Not Be in Charge

OK. It's time for the children to leave the room. The policies that follow the assumption that the world is overpopulated are evil to the core, which is why we must mention them here. In short:

- *Abortion.* What better way to limit a growing population than stripping defenseless children out of the wombs of their mothers? To think this is justified in "progressive" societies makes our stomachs churn. Such countries as China have been heralded by progressives for their mandated-abortion policies. Population control activists turn their heads to the practice of strapping mothers down and killing the little lives inside of them.

- *Forced Sterilization.* It is one thing when a mother or father voluntarily restricts the possibility of having children. We challenge that idea, understanding all the while that it's not an immoral one. But there are countries forcing sterilization on their people. And it didn't end with the Nazis in World War II. Involuntary sterilization has been going on for years in underdeveloped countries.
- *Eugenics.* Scientific experimentation on human reproduction stems from the hideous eugenics movement of old. In the name of twisted science, aborted fetuses are harvested for stem cell research.

All of these awful realities follow in the wake of population control theory. If the actions these theories produce don't convince you, we're not sure what will. Rebut the premise from the get-go: Overpopulation is a myth. The world's resources are plentiful and available. It is a worthy stance, especially when considering the policy solutions of your adversaries.

Our hope is that someday men will look back at the practices of the 20th and 21st centuries and ask the same questions we now ask of previous centuries. *How could they have justified such atrocity?* We ask this of slavery, how a free nation could allow the buying and selling of human beings. It is with the same blindness that we justify the restriction of the birth of children. Human life is devalued through both practices, and always illogically so. We don't buy their bag of goods, and neither should you.

Children Do Not Damage the Environment

We spent the entire 2009-10 school year studying the environment. Two of our daughters were debate partners in the homeschool leagues, and I (Chris) had the privilege of publishing the best-selling debate briefs on the year's topic of environmental policy. Needless to say, I wish these high school debaters were in charge, for they apparently know much more about environmental policy than our elected officials.

Laymen, likewise, don't know environmental science. Like politicians they believe what the experts tell them. This is the catch-22 of the environmental movement in the last 20 years: The complexity of the science allows faulty claims to go unchecked. Laymen—hardworking moms and dads who simply want to raise their children—have little time to expose faulty science. So they take the experts at their word.

The scientific community makes the claim that human beings are a liability to the environment. This claim is false. It is absolutely not true. And recent scandals have unveiled how respected scientists in positions of power have conspired to manipulate scientific data to show rises in global temperature that did not exist. It was fraud, plain and simple, one that true scientists should gladly bring into consideration. Yet despite the public disclosure of hacked e-mails that displayed the vulgar abuse of scientific data, these so-called scientists continue teaching in American and British universities.

Most if not all the environmental scariness—global warming, climate change, oil spills, deforestation, acid rain, rising ocean levels, etc.—are false claims. And we've personally laughed at them for years.

Not everyone laughs along with us, of course. We've had conversations with young couples who cannot believe we take the alarmist claims so lightly. There are couples who actually believe that their voluntary barrenness is doing the climate a favor. They look at us and say, "What do you mean you don't believe in global warming? *How do you know?*" So, for a moment, let's take this question seriously:

We don't know. When a scientist (or a politician posing as a scientist) claims the world should create an economy of carbon credits, we don't take him at his word, and a good scientist never should. Science is built on healthy questioning, not dogmatism. Science is (or should be) all about experimentation. Make a claim, test it, publish its conclusion. This is an incredibly persuasive model that works well with anyone, especially laymen.

Instead, we are shamed into accepting unproven claims. "*How do you know* ocean levels aren't rising?" the young couple will ask us. "How do you know they are?" is our rebuttal. At this point they typically refer to Al Gore's *An Inconvenient Truth,* an article in National Geographic or a news program that showed homes falling into the ocean. We respond with the fact that we had just visited a beach in southern California where, for the first time since 2000, the water was at the same level as it was a decade previous.

We then explain the scientific theory of displacement. Most know the argument: An ice cube melts in a full glass of water, and the water spills over because ice expands. The polar ice caps, if they were melting, would cause that San Diego waterline to rise. Images of polar bears on floating glaciers don't convince us, nor do claims from (even) a U.S. vice president. Polar bears have always enjoyed floating glaciers. Ocean erosion happens. It always has. And camera shots of houses falling off cliffs is an example of poor housing development, not melting ice caps.

This is where the argument should stop. True science trumps emotionalism. The burden of proof is on the scientific community, and the scientific community has conceded the burden to the likes of Mr. Gore. All scientific claims need to be supported; when they aren't, these claims should be dropped. It's simple. Continuing the argument isn't science, it's stupidity. The burden to prove claims rests in the scientific community, and they haven't convinced us. In fact, they have convinced us that some of them will manipulate the data to gain traction for their claims.

But then, dogmatists *rarely* depend on science to prove their claims. They resort to elitism. Credentials are often heralded as the ultimate authority. So-and-so has a PhD in climatology, so we have to accept what he has to say. Remember Paul Ehrlich? Despite his half-century of false predictions, he's still a highly credentialed defender of environmental activism. His best defense is that he has a PhD.

Parents have been propositioned with this line for decades, yet they still fall for it. Why? The answer is strangely close to the same reason people reject the blessing of children. Modern day climatologists resemble snake oil salesmen in how they use their persuasive powers to instill fear in their buyers. When emotional fear is accepted, you'll buy and believe anything.

We remember being taught in grade school that the world, in fact, was cooling. A coming ice age was eminent, a "fact" that *Newsweek* made much of in its April 28, 1975, issue.[9] But global cooling wasn't the only farce that assailed our young minds, disguised as science. We recall being told that the lakes of the Upper Midwest and Canada were acidifying due to the irresponsible pollution of industries. The claims were pounded again and again into every small preschool brain so that we'd all be terribly afraid of the harmful effects of pollution. Today, Minnesota and Canada have the best bass fishing in the world.

Every decade seems to go through its own scary, doom-and-gloom scenarios. In the '90s, the tropical rain forests were on a course for destruction, and the entire West was degenerating into a desert wasteland. Today the jungles of Brazil are just as thick as ever. Remember the evils of Y2K? Be honest, some of you still have wax candles in the basement, leftovers from your stockpiling preparation of certain disaster. For the past several years, every bird flu outbreak has a predicted course of wiping out one-fifth of the world's population. It never does.

Parents should push against any theory, idea or even apparent scientific finding that flaunts its arrogance by posing as a fearmonger. Because the element consistent with all of these doomsday scenarios is *fear*. Fear and change, that is. And usually change that involves money to invest, lives to change and freedom to surrender. Fear is a tool to control the masses, and it is precisely what is evident in the environmental movement.

One of the most revealing comments about the global warming movement came from Al Gore when he was promoting his movie, *An Inconvenient Truth*. In response to some who were doubting his findings, he responded, "The scientists are virtually screaming from the rooftops now. The debate is over!"

The debate is over? You mean, there is no room for discussion or questioning or doubting? That's exactly what he meant, and that's anything *but* science. A continual skepticism of the facts is what threads through proper science, and the first person to claim the debate is over should be immediately thrown headlong from the scientific "community." Today global warming activists are lacing their speeches with the phrase "climate change." What a convenient position. Just a few years ago we were at DEFCON 4 because of rising ocean levels and heatstroke, but now we're faced with global cooling patterns. Again.

This isn't science. This is fanaticism, with advocates clinging to disproved hypotheses beyond any sense of reason. Parents who plan their family based on these frightful theories are playing into a hoax, a most certain lie. Children are not warming the planet any more than jumping fish are creating a tsunami.

This may come as a shock, but we're not friends with many environmentalists. They grow annoyed—or perhaps bored—with what we like to talk about. And we're not interested in talking about claims we know are based on false premises. Instead of an environment we cannot change ourselves, we enjoy talking about the environment that we can. While environmentalists thought for some time that using roll-on deodorant would help close the hole in the ozone layer (another alarm from the scientific community that's led nowhere), we think bringing children into the world, building a family and teaching our young to love and trust God are infinitely more valuable to the world.

Funny, isn't it? Environmental alarmists cling to the pettiest things to validate their human existence. They drive hybrids to show their awareness, choose paper (or better yet, cloth) instead of plastic and use pump hair spray instead of aerosol. They have few to no children, and their thoughts are filled with how they're contributing to the global community in a healthy, functional way. They'll grow old, alone, thinking their contribution meant something. *And they'll be living off the Social Security my kids will be paying in.*

Wendy drives a 15-passenger van and I own the largest SUV ever made, a Ford Excursion. We are birthing the next generation of innovators, creators, businesspeople and entrepreneurs. If you do the math, you'll see that the one guy driving his hybrid to work wastes more gallons of gas *per person* than our heaping helping of humanity does crowded into our gas guzzlers. We are conservationists, not environmentalists. And population control for us means buying a new youth rifle for one of our hunting-age kids—and then using it to target one of those "ghost elks" in the Colorado Rockies.

In the end, our creativity is what measures us. It's that "image of God" trait of which we keep speaking. Through faith and ingenuity, we have the freedom to create our own environments. We have such incredible power to create the environment around us, a power beyond any other creature on the planet. In marriage, a loving couple is able to create human beings—aptly called *miracles*—and the creativity just grows from there. We build shelters, we form communities, we participate in the marketplace of ideas to continue to grow ourselves and grow our provision for our children. Miracles of provision and creativity and prosperity are so numerous that we often take them for granted. So we throw off the adversaries that say our heritage is harming the earth, as should every parent.

---

5 - Fear of Childbirth

"I have set before you life and death, blessings and curses. Now choose life, so that you and your children may live" —Deuteronomy 30:19

Fear encircles the root of the idea that children will harm the environment. But this emotion goes much deeper for most of us than just generating faulty ideologies. We know that we as parents should overcome our fears and be the strong leaders of our families. And we know that this starts with refusing to participate in environmental extremism, raising children who think scientifically and rationally about family and their individual contribution to the world's environment.

But even if you reject the fearmongers, there is still lingering fear for young couples. Ask most people what the opposite of faith is and you'll most likely get this obvious—though incorrect—answer: *doubt.* In our opinion, there is little wrong with genuine doubt. Doubt is a basis for science and can be quite helpful in the development of faith. The opposite of faith, then, is fear, because fear immobilizes our walk with God.

Imagine "Fear" as an animal. It is a snake. Its sole purpose is to creep into your life and cripple you. While you may desire to have faith that moves mountains, Fear reminds you of the realities, the crumbling world out there, the uncertainty of chance, and especially your personal shortcomings. Anything it takes for you to refuse God's calling, Fear will use. Fear lies; it's in its nature to do so. When people turn their hearts from faith, Fear fills the leadership role, and it cradles those it deceives.

Followers of Christ have these two before them: faith and fear. The first holds genuine and exciting life, the deep and profound plan God has for each of our families. The second holds death, not valiant or glorious, but rather dark and bland, unexciting and empty. Metaphorically, God is Love (1 John 4:16) and Satan is Fear. God's love for us wants us to press on through the thick and thin and embrace the plan He has for our lives. Satan, out of his hatred for us, wants us to wallow in our fear and degradation as far from God's plan as he can keep us.

True Christian faith finds no growth in fear. Some believers see Satan around every corner. We don't. Yet when parents elevate their fears above the blessings God may have in store for them, we can't help but see how their lack of faith is a sinister snake, very much a demon they've allowed to coil around their lives.

We constantly come up against fear when speaking with couples and their decision to have—or not to have—children. Though God is pounding on their hearts to have another child—or even their first one—they come up with all sorts of reasons against. And they go far beyond the loony sky-is-falling reasons. Parents *appear* to cling to "rational" fears (overpopulation, harm to the environment, economic instability) that they believe should prompt smaller families. Dig a little deeper, though, and we see that their fear is more crafty than that.

Fear has become the status quo, the popular mindset. And it's difficult to move against the tide of popular sentiment, especially when we've been raised with it. Our educational system constantly drills these fears into our society. This is one of the reasons we choose to homeschool. I (Chris) taught as a public school teacher from 1993 to 2000, and I saw little more than worldview indoctrination in many classrooms. It appears that little has changed since then. Recently a generous relative bought our children an assortment of popular magazines. Even in the classics, such as *Ranger Rick* and *National Geographic Kids*, we could barely turn a page without encountering a rant or a sigh about the evils of global warming or population growth. After a few good laughs and lessons in how deceived the popular media is, the magazines got discarded.

Fear, fear, fear. No wonder parents don't want to bring more children into this falling, crumbling world. And Christians aren't automatically immune to this. Even good ones who actually *read* their Bibles fall into this trap. We've been in Bible studies with God-fearing couples whose knees would shake at the prospect of having children. "Why?" we ask them. And they answer with some gibberish about the end of the world coming soon. More fear, and from the very people who should be fearless.

That's why we have been extremely disappointed to see some Christian leaders jump on the environmental bandwagon. They fall for the premise that "good stewardship" (the biblical root of environmental concern) equates to liberal political advocacy. But that popular advocacy actually responds to nothing more than the great fear that the earth is on the verge of being destroyed by mankind. And *that* leads to some pretty extraordinary stands: The very air we exhale (CO_2) has now been determined a pollutant by the Environmental Protection Agency. Keep this book; a few generations from now people will look at such ridiculousness in the same way we all now see the leech bleedings of the 1800s.

Do you see how Fear is smiling? It's winding itself ever more tightly around its prey, and its ploys are festering. It doesn't matter how irrational these positions are. As long as couples see themselves and their children as taxing to society and the environment, refraining from having children makes sense. Though Scripture says, "As for you, be fruitful and increase in number; multiply on the earth and increase upon it" (Genesis 9:7), Fear worms its way in and persuades us otherwise. It hisses, *Be unfruitful and keep from multiplying.*

When pressed, honest, biblically minded Christians cannot ignore the biblical mandate of *multiplying.* Childbearing is never referenced as some *choice* parents intellectually plan out like a family purchase. It's sad, but couples today get more excited about the purchase of an entertainment system than the expectation of a coming child. Bringing children into the world is a heartfelt conviction backed up with biblical precedent. God wrote it down for us to read and believe and apply. "God blessed them and said to them, 'Be fruitful and increase in number; fill the earth and subdue it'" (Genesis 1:28). Nothing in Scripture ever took away the importance of a family heritage, and nothing in today's culture should convince us otherwise.

God *may* call *some* Christian parents to limit the size of their families. And we won't stand in the way of that. But we clearly believe that He's not calling as many as seem to think so. Most families, we believe, have succumbed to modern, secular thinking rather than submitted themselves to God's will for their lives. They certainly don't have 21st-century cultural persuasions to *resist* in the process. So we say this to you if you believe God wants you to stick with just one or two—or none: Read the rest of this book. Honestly put your convictions to the test on the issue of loving another child, because the rest of the world definitely isn't challenging your ideas of resistance. *Our* ideas, meanwhile, are tested, mangled and maligned from every angle, every day. Yours are embraced and eulogized. So make really and truly sure that they're not lingering out of laziness— out of conformity to the ideas that so easily surround you.

More often, we believe, the true dilemma is for those who feel the conviction *to have children,* yet they face in every corner of their lives (including church) pressure to restrain their (crazy!) conviction. So we throw our support behind moms and dads who feel conviction from God to have children. We say, Go for it! And we'll try to help you as you do.

Fear is a slimeball. And when Fear penetrates our personal lives, our past experiences and our psychologically dysfunctional depths, it has much greater success in controlling our family size. This is where Fear does its mastery work. So fight back with both facts and faith. We've already touched on a couple of areas in which Fear is famous, particularly poverty and harm to the environment. But for many there is deeper fear in the unknown, health problems, change, vulnerability and even the longing for love. These fears keep us from having and loving children. And they are more sinister than the academic fears; they grab for our hearts instead of our minds. Even hard-core environmentalists overcome their logical fallacies and have a child or two, but couples who have their hearts wrapped around personal fear would never dare. They are immobile. These fears, like all fear but the fear of God Himself, should be identified and thrown behind us as we confidently walk in the will God has for us.

We May Not Have a Healthy Child!

This is not uncommon: Parents fear an unhealthy child. We've certainly felt it. Would we be able to handle a special needs child, or a physically handicapped one? We don't like to think of it because, maybe, God has it in His plan. With God's strength we'd be able to effectively care for an unhealthy child, but we've felt that fear deep down. And we've whispered that humiliating prayer, "Please not us, Lord."

Fifteen children into our journey, we have not had a disabled child. Most would say we've been "blessed" with good health. We stop people who say that and ask, "Are families who have children with health issues *cursed*?" They always backtrack, and it's good that they do. We have witnessed families *blessed* with severely disabled children. So we can't say we are somehow more "blessed" than they.

We pray every night with our children, a tradition to which we are extremely loyal. We pray for Simon, a severely handicapped and mentally disabled child from a former church of ours. We haven't attended for several years and many of our children don't even remember who Simon is. But we frequently receive e-mail notices of Simon being admitted to another hospital, so prayer is definitely needed. It is a sharp judgment, though, to assume that Simon is somehow a liability to his family. Those who know him are encouraged to see his great love and his good character. And, we suspect, his parents would rather choke on their own tongues than say they are hindered by his presence.

Similarly, when we attended a small church start-up (upon first moving to Colorado), we encountered a family that included 4-year-old Benjamin, a Down syndrome child. Our fondest memories of him are when he sang "This Is the Day" in our living room. He danced and danced, the center of attention. That family loved their little Benjamin, and so did his church.

Benjamin died unexpectedly from a virus that attacked his heart. And our hearts, along with his family's, were broken as we buried him in a custom-made coffin. Benjamin's life was priceless, worth so much more than people may think. Certainly it was worth more than what they may *fear*.

We can't help but marvel at those families who "suffer" with unhealthy children. We know several, and none of them agree with the common perception that such parenting is a hardship. To the contrary, they have become staunch defenders of the value of every life. We *believe* in the sanctity of life, but these folks *live* it. Try telling parents of invalids or the mentally disabled that their children are not worth the cost they bring to society, and you'll get a Sarah Palin-style mama-bear rage that'll send you running with your tail between your legs.

In 2009, President Obama joked about his bowling score being worthy of the Special Olympics, and a year later his chief of staff Rahm Emanuel flippantly called his comrades "f---ing retards."[11] Neither seemed to have given much thought to the cruelty and prejudice their comments would convey. Sarah Palin, on the other hand, had been forced by life to think quite a lot about such things. And she responded by voluntarily giving birth to a Down syndrome child even though her political career was beginning to roar.

Consider Palin's plight for a moment. She was already the mother of four healthy children, a tally higher than most families. She ascended to the highest position in her home state: governor of Alaska. She enjoyed favorable poll results unparalleled for second-term governors, largely because of her insistence to clean up corruption and instill sound economic policies. And then she got pregnant. And then she discovered the possibility of her carrying a Down syndrome child.

What would conventional wisdom suggest she do? Abortion would have arguably been good for Sarah's career and future. A Down child would seem to naturally thwart any future ambition.

And the toll the child would have on her other children would be great. Demented as it seems, shouldn't Mrs. Palin consider the detriment to society the child would inevitably become?

Sarah and her husband, Todd, gave such thoughts little time and gratefully gave life to Trig. The result? They were blessed beyond their dreams. And they became a national encouragement to families in the same situation as them with handicapped and disabled children. Actually, we believe the Palins are an encouragement to *every* family who bravely loves another child: Every child is a blessing, even when the child comes with handicaps.

There is still that fear in our hearts, though, isn't there? The fear that we couldn't handle what the Palins walked through. But we can. We can! If God chooses to bless us with a disabled child, we will embrace him or her. All the prenatal tests in the world wouldn't change our minds. In fact, we routinely opt out of the ones doctors encourage us to take. The results wouldn't change our minds anyway.

The Palins—together with millions of parents with Down children—argue that they come with *more* blessing. We can only imagine. Seeing the Palin children take care of Trig during their mom's 2008 race for the vice-presidency was inspiring. It wasn't fake. Mom made her decision to have the baby when national politics wasn't even on her radar. She was at the top of her political climb (or so she probably thought), 40 years old, nothing but moose hunting and good times ahead. Trig came and changed all that, and we suspect the Palin family would be the first to say it was for the better.

It's Complicated!

There are so many parents who have one or two children and desire to have more, but have been restricted from having more due to medical complications. "We would have loved to have more children, but ..." What follows when we're told this are details of a medical history that keeps them from having children. It's heartbreaking to hear from moms and dads who desired more children but were left with the disappointing reality of medical malfunctions.

This fear may be one of the most real fears out there. So we gently and compassionately preface all that we say here with a *strong* disclaimer: *We're not medical experts.* We haven't any degree in the sciences nor the obstetrics fields. We are teachers and researchers and writers who don't speak to this issue with the same authority as others could. So we appeal to others to substantiate our claims.

Furthermore, this is a very emotional subject for some. Countless numbers of women have been told—and they've agreed—that they aren't able to have another child, that they should cut off their childbearing years early. We've met many moms and dads who have well-rehearsed stories of how their medical complications keep them from having more children—and they feel like their hearts have been ripped out. They want so much to love another child, but their medical histories keep them from it.

And there are those who bravely keep trying, suffering loss upon miscarriage loss. You might not think we've had the time, but we too have experienced losses through miscarriage in the past two decades. And so we understand the heartache. After the great expectation of receiving a child grows in your mind and soul, the loss is heartrending. Perhaps you'd think we—with our brood of blessings—wouldn't mourn these losses so much, but we wept when they happened.

That said, this book would not be complete without taking aim at some of the things that are accepted as fact and truth in the world of medicine. Indeed, we believe it is riddled with problems. Parents make the mistake of treating their doctors like ultimate authorities over their bodies and reproductive capabilities. Doctors, likewise, sometimes operate with arrogance as if they *were* the ultimate authority. There is a tension between mothers and doctors that, for various reasons, is real and sometimes results in erroneously restricting parents from having more children.

These common complications are cited by mothers—and supported by doctors—who think they should not bear another child:

"I've had Cesarean sections."

It is common practice in medicine to require C-sections for all subsequent deliveries after a mother has had one. But it is not necessary. One-third of all deliveries today end up in C-section, far too many than is needed, some medical experts argue. Removing your baby surgically should be reserved only for emergencies, but it has become something of a common practice for hospital births.

My (Wendy's) older sister had four children, all C-section, and after the fourth she was told to have no more. A friend—a nurse—was told the same after her first C-section, yet had eight more children (all delivered via C-section). She did the research and took control of her own decisions, something my sister was never allowed to try.

VBAC (vaginal birth after Cesarean section) is a trend that seems to come and go. As recently as five years ago, hospitals were allowing, even encouraging VBAC. The American Congress of Obstetricians and Gynecologists (ACOG) has since come out with literature that, though not necessarily discouraging VBAC, advises against it by citing numerous health risks. Because of this, parents who desire VBAC are either forced to find a supportive provider and put up with the restrictions hospitals will enforce (fetal monitoring, IV, no food or drink, etc., all emergency preparation for a possible operation), or opt for a home delivery.

If you've had a C-section, the chances are good that your next pregnancy will be treated like an emergency. This doesn't need to be a dreadful experience, though. Take charge and make sure this is *your* decision (wife and husband), and you may be surprised at how pleasant the experience can be.[12]

"I've had trouble delivering."

We've heard some of the scariest stories of complications during childbirth. Little can be more devastating than excessive bleeding, near loss of life, or even the death of a child. These stories often scare mothers into sterility, and doctors are always ready and willing to "fix" the problem.

Here's a principle that parallels many of these stories: Doctors gravitate toward the worst-case scenario. Why is this? It's largely because of the sue-happy culture we live in. And medical malpractice suits for obstetricians are greater in number than any other field of medicine. And even if a doctor doesn't let the fear of a lawsuit get into her head, she's naturally going to be looking out for the complications—no matter how small of a concern they may be. By doing so, she will inevitably scare mothers with her concern. Get a second opinion! And then get a third one from a reputable midwife.

We've become convinced that the state of maternity care—almost exclusively in America—is broken. Sure, there are caring and competent doctors, but they are all operating within a system that does not inherently respect the importance of birth and birthing families. Convenience, efficiency, and avoiding lawsuits all too often take precedence. The maternity care system is also fixated on "doing something," rather than letting the mother do her work naturally. Doctors are trained to react to emergencies, and while that can be helpful when something really does go terribly wrong, it can also invite overreaction to the "normal" travails of natural childbirth. Robert A. Bradley, MD, notes in *Husband-Coached Childbirth,* "A good obstetrician has been defined as one equipped with a broad rear end and the good sense to sit calmly on it and let nature take its course."[13]

Sometimes, even after a delivery goes off without a hitch, doctors will sometimes make the case that having another child should be avoided. Gestational diabetes, high blood pressure, vitamin deficiencies and anxiety are all aggravated with pregnancy. So the going assumption is this: Avoid pregnancy to avoid these problems. Rarely will a doctor prescribe alternative solutions.

Instead of settling, get a good nutritionist to figure out a diet that will help control these problems. The Brewer Diet comes highly recommended for pregnant mothers and has testimonials of several of these ailments disappearing.[14] Low levels of vitamin D in mothers sometimes bring problems, but these are easily remedied by eating cultured dairy products such as cheese and yogurt.

Fatty fish species such as salmon and herring also offer significant amounts of vitamin D.[15]

We know some women whose symptoms actually go away when they get pregnant. A friend who has had 13 children suffers from rheumatoid arthritis, yet her pain goes away when she's carrying a child. She takes aspirin but has never had to resort to strong drugs because of her consistent pregnancies. She bucks doctors who claim, "You should stop because of your arthritis." Why? She's better when she *doesn't* stop. And her household is full of thankful children because of her stubbornness.

Really, though, we don't see her as being the stubborn one. She's done her homework, researched her situation and is confident of her decision. Her husband is an emergency medic, so together they are able to see through the faulty medical advice. Doctors don't have crystal balls to be able to see into your future, though they often give opinions as if they do. Treat their opinions as just that. And never settle for just one. Seek several opinions from doctors, midwives and even other mothers who can identify with your concerns. Chances are great that there are mothers who suffer from the same ailments you do, and the solutions are diverse.

"I've had painful deliveries."

If you have had difficult deliveries, we certainly can understand your fear of childbirth. Nevertheless, the principle of taking charge of your health still stands. Our preferred method of delivery is the Bradley Method. Of the various methods out there, I have found this one to be the most attentive to my body. Besides, an integral part of the delivery is your "coach," the one who is leading you through the pain and the delivery process. The Bradley Method focuses on working with your pain rather than avoiding it, ultimately putting you in charge of the most things possible during delivery.

Here's a misconception about childbirth: Someone or something is going to take away all your pain. Why it is a surprise, I'll never know, but know this: Childbirth is painful. Extremely painful! Don't ever think that the doctor will somehow take the pain away with simple procedures. Women often go to the hospital ill-prepared, somehow expecting a doctor or medical technician to magically make the pain disappear. Such expectations set mothers up for failure. It is a mistake to think such things, but women I've spoken to about their painful experiences typically explain that they didn't *expect* such pain.

Which leads to another misconception: All your deliveries will be the same. I've had 15 deliveries, not two of them exactly the same. I've long since gotten rid of the idea that I have it all figured out and know exactly what's going to happen. I prepare for each childbirth by reading my Bradley book,[17] exercising and eating well, knowing that I've got the rewarding work of childbirth ahead of me. Every mother should be as prepared.

"I always need to be induced."

Inductions nearly always complicate labor, yet are often done to accommodate for a doctor's or parent's schedule. Like C-sections, once an induction happens, doctors will automatically assume another induction is needed. Some doctors insist on it, dredging up illogical scenarios for the poor mother, scaring her into thinking she will be pregnant forever or, worse, she'll die.

Most birth periods cover five weeks—three before and two after. The maternal medical practice has moved this acceptable length of time up and up. We even had one doctor claim he induced at 40 weeks across the board—no exceptions. All but two of my 15 pregnancies have gone over the 40-week mark. But doctors would lay terrible consequences on my heart—like the possibility of stillbirth—if I refused induction. Today it is common practice to require women to schedule induction *before* the 40-week due date—even as early as 35 weeks gestation.

While much of what doctors say can be forgiven, this one angers me. They often leave mothers scared to death about the prospect of delivery. An ultrasound is inevitably used to show the baby measuring larger than average, so the doctor will schedule an induction to *hurry and get that baby out of there!* But ultrasounds can be off by as much as two pounds. So where's the proof that the baby is too large to survive within the mother's womb?

More often than not, an induced delivery turns out to be a miserable one, filled with complications. The story ends with this: "Good thing you delivered in the hospital where we could take care of this emergency!" Perhaps. The natural course never got a chance to weigh a verdict. But our suspicion is this: if the delivery was left to start naturally, things would have likely been fine.

My Doctor Objects!

See how all these common complications and worries weigh on a mom's and dad's decision to love another child? Doctors fear complications almost religiously, like fearing the devil of circumstance around every corner. The science of medicine—once a valiant defender of life—now huddles in fear of complication. What's happened to the brave doctor out to save the life of the patient—the mother and the child—against all odds?

Of course, there are still some noble doctors who work with mothers rather than against them. But they're difficult to find. Of our 15 children, four of them were born in the hospital. The rest arrived at home. The idea of home delivery scares many parents, and we're not necessarily advocating it. Make no mistake, though, home birth has a much higher success rate than hospital birth.[18]

I have had 15 healthy children free (mostly) of complication. When the infrequent complication does arise, Chris and the professional midwives have always been able to work through them quite naturally. Despite this incredible track record, doctors will point to my "multiple pregnancies" as a potential health risk. It's almost laughable. Mothers who have more than, say, four children will inevitably be flagged as a problem no matter how great those previous pregnancies were.

Another common reason for professional concern: age. Any mother over 35 is labeled high-risk. And then those risks are typically overreacted to by monitoring every little issue. Age doesn't mean everything, though, when it comes to how successful a pregnancy will be. In my case, I am much healthier at 42 than I was at 32.

Complications can happen, but childbirth is as natural as the rising sun. It's not an emergency situation. It's childbirth. And maybe that's why we've opted for home delivery instead of hospital delivery. Doctors, unlike midwives, are trained to respond to *emergencies*. So we sincerely believe this is the better choice.

When I am pregnant, my body is a powerhouse, but I'm emotionally fragile. I don't like arguing with my doctor and grow tired of hearing the litany of complications that "could" occur. This fear preys on my emotions, as I believe it does on most mothers'. Ultimately, this fear ends with couples opting out of pregnancy, out of building their family.

A Healthy Perspective on Childbirth

I have had wonderful pregnancies and deliveries. And for the most part, my midwives have heralded my body as "made for having children." Still, for years I fell into thinking that my own health didn't matter. And strange as it sounds, doctors are much more likely to prescribe a pill than a diet, handing out unnatural solutions rather than natural ones.

Not that I put too much blame on the doctors for this one. Who wants to tell a pregnant mother that she's overweight and out of shape? To say that her dietary choices may have led to complications would be nearly impossible news to share, let alone for the emotional mother to receive. It's so much easier to point to uncontrollable reasons (blood pressure, genetics, menstrual history, etc.). A doctor honest enough to tell a mother that her health is the greatest reason for her complications is a doctor to respect, but you probably don't go to him. And if you did, chances are that you'd get angry with him for saying so.

I used to think this way. The years of my greatest complications were in my late 20s and early 30s. I was 50 pounds overweight and could barely bend over to pick up my toddlers. Walking a block would exhaust me, and I could out-eat Chris at dinner. No wonder I felt awful in these years, though no doctor would dare tell me it was because of my personal health. I eventually came to realize I needed to take control of my well-being. This was about me and my daily choices. I needed to slim down, change what I chose to eat, and exercise.[19]

This isn't an easy topic to broach with moms. The wave of excuses rush in and many a mom rides it. The excuses are much easier to live with at times than the reality of making hard health choices. What is most sad is that women limit their family size because they're scared of external complications, refusing to consider the simple dietary choices at their disposal.

What I've discovered is the healthy life; it is wonderful, something I want every mom to relish. Such a life does not exclude childbirth any more than it excludes good eating. Too many mothers think that dietary control is a life of misery. Have you ever said to yourself, "There's nothing you can do. You're a mother who has birthed children, so you're going to naturally be this overweight." Perhaps you try to talk yourself into enjoying it, calling yourself "pleasantly plump" or "proudly carrying the weight of motherhood."

Until you lose your breath just sweeping the floor. Or you can't fit into any of your clothes. When your pregnancy comes, problems kick in right away. Gestational diabetes, high blood pressure, muscle tone issues, bladder infections, severe back pain—all due to your being out of shape to begin with. And dealing with them while pregnant is challenging, to say the least. It's mothers who get these things under control *before* pregnancy who typically enjoy a healthier pregnancy.

So study your situation and get the facts, not just about weight, but about all the fears that factor into loving another child. Families who educate themselves and are honest about their fears of childbirth find ways to overcome them. As a result, they have a much more fulfilling and healthy delivery. They walk confidently in faith and force that snake called Fear to uncoil from around their hearts. It's then that they're often blessed with another child.

6 - Making Love

"Sometimes we must be hurt in order to grow. Sometimes we must fail in order to know. Sometimes we must lose in order to gain. Because some lessons in life are best learned through pain." —Unknown

"Let the wife make the husband glad to come home, and let him make her sorry to see him leave." —Martin Luther

There are two ways a married couple can have sex. You can have as much of it as you want while blocking its natural results by way of birth control or surgical "solutions." If you have one or two children already, you can pour the next 15-20 years into them and still have youthful years left to enjoy the fruits of your hard work. You'll likely be able to afford all the amenities in life that a couple could want, and you'll blend in with the culture. Perhaps you'll even grow old with no regrets.

Or you can embrace your spouse, have as much sex as you want *without* blocking its natural results—and have as many children as God gives you. And that doesn't mean you'll have 15 by the time you're 40! Most couples are not able to conceive as quickly or as easily as the Jeubs. We know of many families who are walking the same path of faith as us, yet they are blessed with few children. Wendy is one of 2 percent of women who is able to continue her cycle within two months of delivering, and, unlike many women, she is able to get pregnant while nursing. Her body was made for having children.

We count that a joy. Our testimony is meant to encourage you to have another child, but not necessarily 15!

In our opinion, the first choice brings much more complication into marriage than the latter. Our marriage bed is liberating; their marriage bed is complicated. We don't get knotted up thinking of the possibility of conception and all the fallible gimmicks available to prevent it. It's unnatural, really, to fight the attraction two married people have for each other, especially at the times when the woman is most fertile. Saying "no" when her body is saying "yes" is painful, yet millions of couples resort to this. This is the way of Natural Family Planning (NFP), abstaining when you want to engage the most. It leads to the popular joke about NFP: What do you call couples who practice NFP? *Parents.* They made love when their bodies demanded it, and they were blessed with a child. We say "amen" to that.

Still, Natural Family Planning is probably the *best* form of contraception. It's all natural, and like most of our views on childbearing, natural is better. We practiced NFP for the first few years of our marriage. We were enthusiastic about it and, for a time, the abstinence side of the practice nurtured our lives and kept our minds on each other. We don't have much to gripe about, then, when it comes to couples engaging in their natural cycles and working with them. Let's not fool ourselves, though. Intentionally avoiding pregnancy is intentionally avoiding a blessing, and these couples should give it a second thought, just as we eventually did.

Though there is something *natural* about NFP, we see little *control* in birth control. Is it control to stop the passion to reach for the condom? That condom is controlling the couple, not the other way around. Maybe we're naive (we haven't thought about these things for years), but we don't envy such marriages. What more emasculating, mood-ruining thing is there than men messing with balloons?

Women have it worse, largely because of the myriad of choices available. They're not freeing; they're confining. The responsibility for couples, especially those *not* in a marriage union, typically lies on the woman to figure it out. Side effects include sporadic bleeding, weight troubles, uncontrollable emotions, blood clots, etc. On and on the pain goes. The pill was heralded as the great liberator of women in its day, but they're not fooling everybody.[20] So the search for the perfect contraception continues, all for the sake of restricting the blessing of a child. Why not just throw all that stuff away, embrace your spouse, and start making babies?

Yet you still pause. You may have logically worked your way through all the "reasons," but you still aren't able to come to terms with the idea of loving another child. It isn't that you don't want another; you genuinely *fear* the prospect. The what ifs creep in and start planting seeds of doubt, like ...

- What if I get fat?
- What if I miscarry?
- What if my spouse decides to leave me?
- What if our other children hate their baby brother?

We've all had friends—perhaps grown people of faith—who apparently abandon their once-unshakable faith in God. More so, we've seen couples split apart. We've known families that embrace the concept of having many children, then break into pieces as a dad or a mom leaves. It's heartrending. These stories shock us, and when children are involved, they deeply sadden us. Some of the stories anger us.

Just in the past three weeks we've heard of three marriages falling apart. These weren't just past acquaintances; these are dear friends with whom we've attended church, shared meals, spent days visiting. I (Wendy) bumped into one friend at Sam's Club, a mom of seven children—one with special needs—to learn that her husband quit his job, moved out of state, and now wants nothing to do with her or his children. Chris found an old friend online—a leader in the homeschool movement—and inquired about his family: His wife divorced him two years ago over "irreconcilable differences." Then, most recently, a mom of seven and one of my dearest friends, left her family out of the blue to move in with an old high school boyfriend. I found out when she un-friended me on Facebook.

What's going on? We're quite certain: We *must* address faith *and* marriage. These two elements have got to be foundational to your family. Without a solid understanding of loving God and your spouse (the Greatest Commandment once again), you will not be able to raise a loving family. We encourage families to have children, and children often ramp up the flames of love you have for each other and for God. However, couples who bring children into unloving and hostile environments are not doing anyone any favors.

That's your final fear, isn't it? Be honest. You secretly fear that you could end up being nothing more than another shocking story. You wonder if your marriage is really that great. You fear that you'll bring children into a dysfunctional mess, perhaps reminiscent of a deficient family upbringing of your own. Your faith can always be stronger, so you reasonably think that you're not ready for the commitment of another dependency. God is important in your life, sure, but you're far from a martyr. You're not sure you're ready to bring another child into the world because, frankly, you're unsure of your own stability. Why bring children into instability?

This has much more to do with *making love* than *making children*. Like wrapping our logic around birth control and avoiding children, we make the mistake of thinking it's all about making sure the pregnancy test comes back positive or negative. It's such shallow thinking. It has everything to do with love—in our hearts and in our marriage. Our relationships start with the love that binds us together, not the children we conceive or those we attempt to avoid.

We had originally titled this book *Have Another Child.* That's what we're trying to persuade you to do, or at least consider. But we discovered that in leaving out the *love* part of the equation we were making a huge assumption about you and your marriage. We were assuming that you already love each other and merely need to get over the cultural assumption that children aren't a blessing. This was backward, the cart before the horse. If you don't have love in your marriage ... *don't* have another child. We want you to *love another child,* not just deliver one. We're into building *families,* not kennels.

Children don't complicate marriages, they edify them. When two people understand and nurture the love they have for each other, children come most naturally. The number of children doesn't make much difference. A home full of love is, well, *lovely,* whether it contains two children or 20. Likewise, a home full of bitterness and despair is ugly for everyone, something we wish upon no one.

We believe families fall apart because of a lack of love. Is there any other reason? Cited in court documents may be the typical things (adultery, alcoholism, abuse), but they are really symptoms stemming from lovelessness. Without fail, the reasons marriages fall apart have absolutely nothing to do with family size. But they have everything to do with the lack of love. In good marriages, love is the fuel that keeps the family growing. When a family has a functional view of love—and that function starts with recognizing love as the most important thing in a family—it is an unstoppable powerhouse.

It's difficult for the two of us to imagine family life without a profound love standing strong at its core. When a husband and a wife are in love, the demands of a household fall into place. There is purpose and joy, and when challenges arise (and they always do) they seem trivial. We've had our low moments in our marriage, but the elements of an unloving relationship—hatred, abuse, ridicule, spite—have never found a place. Our love has seen us through arguments and has given us grace for each other. Ultimately, these low moments turned into opportunities to refine and polish our marriage, growing closer and closer as the years unfolded.

We'll share an inside joke with you for a moment: The best love we've ever made in our marriage has followed bitter arguments. We giggle a little at this, sometimes thinking, "Hey, let's get into a fight. Remember the love we made last time we got into a fight?" Lovemaking is a wonderful way to wrap up offenses, misspoken words and emotional outbursts. Married people shouldn't fight, but when they do, they shouldn't "let the sun go down"[21] till they've made up, tied each other into a knot and had some great sex.

How we wish this was true for others! But we're afraid we're an exception. It is very likely that the biggest hesitation to having more children is the lack of love between husband and wife. Why would a woman want to bring children into the world with a man who's not all that interested in her? Why would a man desire the same when his wife thinks poorly of him?

Love Gone Sour

Let's role-play for a moment to help give a picture of what we're trying to say. The following situation is made up, but the elements of the conversation will likely resonate. We created a fictional couple: John and Sue. They've been married for nearly 20 years and have a modest number of children, two of whom have flown from the nest. They own the perfect little townhome, attend church regularly and are volunteers in the community. Though they appear to be a well-balanced family, Sue doesn't think so. To her closest girlfriends, this is what she says about her husband:

"John is always working, and he can still barely keep his clients happy. When he comes home he's too tired to help me with dishes or laundry. Oh, but he has plenty of energy later when we go to bed, if you know what I mean. I often have to kick him out and make him sleep on the couch. He has an obsession with helping others, always willing to give to people in our church, yet he tells me not to spend too much on groceries. He spends his time fixing up others' homes (he's a contractor), but I can't seem to get him to fix much around here. It's a show he puts on for others. I've known him for 20 years, and he's just a bum."

Little feels more unloving to a man than disrespect. And Sue has slipped into despising hers, letting the little lies that fit her emotions at the time grow into seriously negative opinions.

John, meanwhile, doesn't see things the same way as Sue. His story is quite different. He doesn't have a group of guys he complains to like Sue has a group of girlfriends, but he has one close friend he opens up to, an old buddy from high school. John's complaining goes like this:

"I try to stay out of Sue's way. She doesn't love me, that's for sure, and she sure doesn't submit to me like the Bible says. I don't know what she does all day, but I usually come home to a messy house with her still in pajamas. She expects me to wash dishes and do laundry after I've been slaving all day on worksites. She doesn't respect the hard work I put in to allow her to stay home and take care of the kids. Good grief, she spends money like it grows on trees, and she's never seen a bag of candy she hasn't bought—which, I might add, are showing up all around her, if you know what I mean! Doesn't she know that there's a credit card bill I have to pay every month? I try to love her, I really do, but what's there to love? I could've left her years ago, but I've stuck it out. And the only thanks I get is "go sleep on the couch!" She whines to her girlfriends about what a bum I am, but they don't know how much of a witch she can be."

Little is more insulting to a woman than complaining about her weight. Nothing good ever comes from trying to "fix" a wife's waistline. And John has given up trying to see around it, exposing the ugly reality in his heart: He can no longer see Sue's inner beauty.

As much as Sue *disrespects* John, John doesn't *appreciate* Sue. He takes it for granted that Sue will be there at home, caring for the kids and keeping things going. He zeros in on the shortcomings like what she's buying (junk food) rather than appreciating the fact that she did the shopping at all. How typical is the scenario of a husband sitting to eat dinner only to complain about how something was cooked.

Sound familiar? We wish it didn't. But our suspicion is that there are elements in John and Sue's situation that are far too common in families. Should they divorce? We're certain you could find a psychologist ready and willing to write this marriage off as "long gone." But Scripture gives only one reason for divorce: infidelity. Is the situation between John and Sue hopeless? We actually see a lot of hope in it. Love can penetrate this marriage and, within a year, they could be *in* love again, just like they were when they were young.

John and Sue are caricatures, of course. But its their disrespect for each other that's the real joke. Their lack of love is downright humiliating. And though they're not having affairs, they're as unfaithful as those who do.

This book is mostly written in the plural possessive: Chris and Wendy Jeub speaking as one. But in this chapter we're going to split our words into two voices to better deal with John and Sue:

Wendy's Words to Sue

John's right, Sue! You're not submitting to your husband as the Bible says. And never mind that the submission in John's mind is probably not the submission of the Bible. "Wives, submit to your husbands as to the Lord," the Apostle Paul writes in Ephesians 5:22. It's such a roadblock verse for most wives, but I see it much differently than most people. I submit *in love* to my husband. Submission without love is ugly, abusive, controlling and manipulative. I submit to Chris like a student submits to her teacher. And that idea of being a student has carried me farther than you might think.

Study your husband. Know him, research him, get into him. Talk with him when he feels like talking, and observe him when he doesn't. Fill your thoughts with how to please him, how to nurture him, how to love him. Resist thoughts that are self-serving or demanding.

But Sue, being a student of your husband does *not* include manipulation. You're manipulating your man when you try to change him. You knew him when you married him, so don't try to change him now. Instead, *love* him. Stop trying to get him to do dishes and fold laundry, and *never* keep yourself from him physically to manipulate him. If you want something from your husband, just ask. Maybe even ask two or three times. But don't use sex to get it. Or worse: keep sex from him when you feel that you don't.

I talk to a lot of women who try to convince me that if they just had a different husband it would be so much easier to be submissive, to love. Such a thought is an insult to your husband and an incredibly cruel thing to think. You keep thinking like that and you'll find yourself divorced faster than you can cry "alimony," and the "cool dude" you'll have as a replacement will be half the man you have now. So hold your husband up to be the best husband he can be. What does that look like? You find things to compliment him on. You focus on the positive. You turn the other cheek to the negative. Notice and praise the things he does that you like. Pay attention and give him good feedback. He deserves it—whether you think he does or not!

Keep your tongue from being a sword. Your complaints about your husband's hard work are bullets that shoot him down. You're choosing to be irritated by the very things that are your husband's greatest gifts to you. Refuse to think of these things as negatives.

Insisting that they annoy you is the most unloving thing you can do to your husband. You are slicing into the very fabric of who he is.

I know what you're thinking, Sue. I can see it all over your face. If you love him like this—if you submit to your man—you'll get walked on, taken advantage of. But this is an incredible deception; don't fall for it. You have it within your power to instill greatness in him. When you start to change your mind and attitude toward your husband, to see him as the man God created him to be, you will see the blessings and the benefits of loving him for who he is.

Treat your husband the way you want to be treated. The Golden Rule applies to marriage just as much if not more than to your friendships. This is an act of sacrificial love. And because it is, it will turn his heart toward you, too. My amazing husband loves to leave his dirty jeans on the floor every night. It annoys me. But I have vowed to overlook it. I will pick up his jeans a thousand times rather than turn something as simple as dirty laundry into a burr in our marriage.

So easily I could badger him: "It's so inconsiderate of you! Why can't you learn!" But where would that get me? It would get me tied into knots ... for nothing. Truth be told, you can get upset over *anything*. You can be upset that it's cloudy outside, but ranting and raving won't do a thing to change it. Why choose to be upset with your spouse, then? It's an old, old cliché, but why make mountains out of molehills?

Perhaps you're thinking that your marriage is much worse than mine, so you're justified in your spite. But even if it *is* worse—and I'd ask you to question whether that's reality or just piqued perception— it's never so bad that love can't penetrate it and make it good. Love has a miraculous way of figuring out how to make it all work.

So becoming a student of your husband is not a chore, a duty or something that enslaves you, Sue. Quite the contrary, it is freeing. When you become a student of your husband, you will discover joy in your marriage and, perhaps, your husband's strengths will start to come out and you'll see a much bigger man than you ever thought possible.

Have you forgotten that your husband *is* a man? And that men really do think differently than women? We women often think like a spider web: Everything comes into contact with everything else. Men aren't usually like this. Men run one thought program at a time. That's why when you talk to him while he's working in the garage he can't recall what you said. Don't yell at him for not listening. Start understanding *how* he listens. Ask him again later when you have his full attention!

And never forget this: You're married to a faulty person. Maybe that's the first thing I've said that you agree with. And I'll grant you it. But I'll counter with, *Who isn't?* Your husband is married to one, too, Sue. We are all faulty people, which is why we need a Savior. Love overlooks the negatives and focuses on the positives. Can you be a student of your husband? Before you said "I do" you were. Do it again, then. Let him be the *man* in your life.

Chris Calls Out John

OK, John, maybe your gripe is legitimate. Your wife is nagging you to do the dishes and laundry. I'd go nuts if my wife nagged me to pick up my own laundry. (I can't believe she shared that story!) So I feel for you, John. Especially that she tears you down in front of her friends. She disrespects you. Man, I feel for you.

But you're *demanding* her submission. Did you know that submission is required of husbands, too? You're banging the very verse over her head that you need to practice, too: "Submit to one another out of reverence for Christ" (Ephesians 5:21). And a few verses later, you're commanded to give this idea substance: "Husbands, love your wives" (Ephesians 5:25). Friend, you cannot miss on this one.

You're making the mistake most men make: You're showing your love in sacrifice, work and provision. You expect Sue to see this for what it is—sacrifice, hard work and provision. Keep doing this, for it's an act of love. But another act of love is overlooking the bitterness, the attacks, the arrows that come your way. John, let it go, don't take Sue's attacks personally.

You are called to lead, and having to remind her who's the boss is far from great leadership. Sue's not the only one who needs to become a student again. You must learn what makes her tick. Be gentle with her, not demanding.

You're not the only man in the world to be faced with a few dirty dishes, John. A woman who always pushes routine chores to the top of her honey-do list may be hard to deal with, but a man whose masculinity is threatened by sudsing up his hands is, quite frankly, stupid. I'll tell you what: The next time you come home to a dirty kitchen with a wife in pajamas, tell her you're going to do those dishes and watch the kids while she gets some "her time" showering and freshening up. I'd put money down that you're going to have a great evening after the kids are in bed.

The point is simpler than you think: A woman falls in love with a man who truly loves her. A man who serves her. You can't slice and dice your service, restricting it to certain times of the day. In all your work, in and out of the home, be Sue's provision. Be her *man*.

And you have got to start appreciating her. You complaining about her weight or her pajamas is nitpicking and terribly unattractive. Look past those things and see the beauty you married. Appreciate her like you did back in the day. She's taking care of the family while you provide for her and the children. This union can be so incredible, but it has to start with your appreciating what she does at home.

A great way to do that is to come home and talk over her day. Sue wants to let you know about all she's done. So little of what a women does in the home *stays* done. So it's good for her to tell you what she's accomplished—when she's accomplished it. Give her a safe place where she can download her day. Otherwise it feels to her like it's all bottled up and doesn't count for much. Come on, is listening to her talk about her day for 10 minutes really that hard?

There's a reason she's still in her PJ's, by the way. It's because she's been busy! Just like you don't want her to disregard your hard work, don't disregard hers. Especially if you have small children, it's very stressful to spend 10 hours watching over their every waking moment. Don't underestimate her time out with the ladies either. She needs this time away from the kids to recharge her internal batteries. Trust me, if she gets too "run down" there's a good chance she'll turn on you in ways you haven't even seen yet. Help her by kicking her out the door for a break. And here's another tip: Knock her socks off by having the kids in bed and the house cleaned up when she gets home.

John, you've gotta love Sue like Christ loves the church. He gave Himself up for her, and you need to do the same. Take the shots she throws, my friend, but don't return them. Christ focuses on our strengths, even if we aren't deserving.

Changing Marriage With Love

If your marriage resembles John and Sue's, you likely have a heart of rock right now, and you're refusing to give in. Why? Because giving in hurts. Submission is vulnerability. Knives in the back, stakes in the heart, *nails in the hands.* These are the consequences of submissive love. But you know what? *It's worth it.* Because nobody can keep throwing those knives, driving those stakes or pounding those nails forever into a spouse who willingly accepts them without a whimper and with love in his eyes. John and Sue *can* learn to love each other. Neither of them needs to find a new mate. And if they do, they'll likely end up in the same frustrating situation a few years down the road. Instead, they need to submit to each other, become students of each other, love each other.

Here's what John and Sue are telling their friends one year later:

Sue: "I can't wait till John comes home tonight. I'm getting the house cleaned up so we can go out on our date. He's been working hard on a difficult job, one where the owner isn't too happy with him, so I'm going to treat him like the king he is. If the house is clean, he can spend time with the kids while I do my hair up nice. The laundry will have to wait till tomorrow, or the kids can fold it while we're gone. It'll give them something to do. Hopefully the kids will be asleep when we get home later, because the night will only be *half* over by then."

John: "I am so glad I have a good wife to come home to. This guy I'm working for is being a pain; I can't wait till the project is over. But I'll betcha Sue has something up her sleeve for me tonight. Lately, she's really made me feel like a real man when my job hits me hard. And, boy, is she looking fantastic lately! I hope I can get this project done this week so I can move on to something that pays a little more. That way maybe we can fix up those things around the house like she's been wanting. Sue deserves better, and she's put up with enough excuses. I'm outta here, man. I gotta get home to my bride!"

We gave a talk similar to this in Colorado at a homeschool conference two years ago. We weren't polished; we actually read most of it from our typewritten notes. But when we looked up from our notes, we saw many parents crying, some even sobbing. We were touching a nerve—among a ballroom full of Christian homeschool parents, of all people. The Johns and Sues are plentiful in our society. It's no wonder divorce is so common, even among Christians.

There are three important things to notice with our role-play. First, the situations don't make any difference. John's and Sue's *attitudes* needed to change first. When we talk with couples who have marital problems, the problems seem like the world to them, but they are rarely the biggies you'd think they would be. Wives often make the pettiest things out to be mighty betrayals—on par with even adultery. Husbands tend to get used to their wives freaking out, then deal with it by turning into a dopey clown who never takes his wife's true feelings into consideration. What an ugly cycle.

So that change of attitude is the first show of love. Love "keeps no record of wrongs" (1 Corinthians 13:5). The best marriages carry this element of love. Petty things remain petty. The motto of love resembles a popular saying out there: "Don't sweat the small stuff." We've heard people follow that up with: "And it's all small stuff." Retrieve that bit of wisdom the next time your spouse irritates you. Choose to overlook the irritation.

The second thing: When you love someone, you often will see weaknesses as strengths. Sue used to think that her husband was a bum, but his success was hindered by a nagging wife. John used to think that his wife was a witch, but she was an abandoned woman whose husband did not appreciate her. What they thought was a spiral downward was a turn upward with the injection of love.

It's strange. So often the things that end up irritating us about our spouse are the very things we used to admire about them. I (Chris) had a friend who was an avid hunter. He took me hunting my first year in Colorado and taught me much of what I now know about Colorado elk hunting. The guy loved hunting and loved teaching others (like me) how to do it. This was his strength, very likely one his wife was originally attracted to before marriage. Now married, though, she beat him down every time he'd come home from a trip. "If you cared about me as much as you cared about hunting ..." she'd say. They eventually divorced. He now writes books and continues to organize hunts for others. I suppose you could argue that now he's "free" from his former wife and able to fly with what God has been calling him to do. I think differently: What a powerful man he would have been if his wife was the encourager she refused to be.

I (Wendy) had a friend who was the picture-perfect wife. She birthed three children with her husband and made sure their home was immaculate. She didn't ask for much from her husband, but he hardly appreciated her efforts. He would ridicule her spending and even sleep with the checkbook under his pillow. He always assumed she would be there for him, but one day she gathered her stuff and left. He was—with all the children—dumbfounded and shocked. She had found someone who finally appreciated her and, in adultery, left her husband for this other man. All the apologizing in the world wouldn't get her back, and the two are now preparing for divorce.

We're not excusing either of these two situations. Both resulted in children being torn between two parents as a godly heritage was stripped away. Both families have beautiful children, and it breaks our hearts to see them being deprived of loving parents. They're making the best of their new lives, but how sad it is that love found no room in their first.

Both of these situations ended in something we hate: *divorce.* They gave up loving each other and embraced bitterness, spite and anger for each other. Count this as a lesson for you and your marriage. Your spouse has wonderful strengths that you should be in the habit of meditating on, caressing and encouraging. If your habit is ridiculing and belittling, you may end up just as our friends did—divorced. Your marriage will certainly not be a loving one.

This leads to the last thing to notice: hope. Couples *can* discover the joys of love in a marriage. It is almost a surprise to a husband and a wife how easy it is to love each other, submit to each other and become students of each other. John and Sue are now happy and in love. And she's a better homemaker for it. He's a better contractor. Love has been restored to their family, and what a joy their marriage now is. Instead of bearing down on each other and exaggerating each other's faults, they get into each other and explore each other's feelings, thoughts and emotions. Their relationship continues to build. The sky is the limit for them. They're on cloud nine, and things are only going to get better. A lifetime together with a marriage full of this kind of love is too short.

It is this kind of love that bears children. Think about it. The act of making love—when it is in total submission to each other and totally selfless—is the act that conceives children. What a perfect illustration of God's creation. The best sex on this planet is between a husband and wife who are completely vulnerable and completely giving. From this act of love come the miracle of children.

7 - One

"Freedom exists for the sake of love." —Pope John
Paul II

It's no surprise that so many divorced couples point to finances as the reason. Money was a point of contention early in our marriage. Wendy handled the finances, and rather liked the control. Formerly a single mom knowing what it was like to live on her own, she was naturally more cautious, more responsible. I (Chris) had a rack of student loan debt, and she handled paying off this debt much better than I. This seemed like a good way to kick off our marriage: Wendy in charge of the money, me focused on working for it. Seemed good to go, so let's have some kids!

After a few children, though, our agreement on how to handle the finances started to wobble. Wendy continued to be cautious—perhaps overly cautious—and would grow frustrated over my purchases. I felt I was never able to work hard enough or make enough, and I felt henpecked when I purchased *anything*. A wedge began to form in our marriage.

Finances became our divider; the blessing of money turned into a curse. Paying bills every month was a dreaded chore. We tried to do it together, to balance our budget and count out the meager amount of money left between the two of us. But our attempts often led to frustration and arguments. So one day I took it all away from Wendy. Not the money itself, just the weight of it. And it wasn't an immature power grab—she'll vouch for that! Rather, it was a relief to her. I just swept the responsibility from her and said, "Enough is enough, this is something I have to do for this family."

At first it was a bit scary. There was mistrust and suspicion that I would spend us into debt we wouldn't be able to get out of. Yet I trusted Wendy's input, and I would regularly seek out her ideas and her considerations in family purchases. Wendy continued her frugal habits, always shopping for the bargains, listening carefully to my concerns about whether we were spending too much or being too tight. She wasn't knotting herself up with worry about finances anymore, though. And since I was the one "in charge," my own frivolous purchases became fewer and fewer. I now had firsthand knowledge of where the money was coming and going, and that was a sobering responsibility.

It could have just as easily gone the other way, had we been wired differently. We've seen couples go the exact opposite direction and do fine. The late Larry Burkett, a financial counselor whose books we read early in our marriage to help get a grip on our finances, was the overly cautious one in his marriage. You'd think the financial counselor would have control of the family checkbook, but he didn't. His wife did. This wasn't a threat to his masculinity at all, though. Nor did it abdicate his leadership. Their arrangement worked much better that way, and they happily grew old together.

See how this dance goes? The man leads, the woman follows, and the couple dances the night away. The more my wife trusts me, the more I appreciate her. And the more she empowers me, the more I love her. She graciously follows my lead, and I strive all the more to lead with love. What a beautiful dance our marriage has been for 20 years now. And we're looking forward to bigger and better years in the future.

Marriage, if you haven't noticed by now, is the perfect environment to love another child. It is beautiful, romantic, devoted and loving. It's where family starts.

The Family Unit

Let's put the idea of "family" into perspective. The family is the organized body of people that—unlike any organized body mankind can put together—is nearly unbreakable by outside forces. Sure, divorce messes that up, but family structures are still solid. Compare contractual unions (man-made) with siblings (born into it) for a moment. Governments are fragile and leadership inevitably fails us, but brothers and sisters are largely inseparable. Only extremely secular individuals belittle family bonds, especially the bond between a parent and a child. Ever try to explain how much love a parent has for his or her child to someone who doesn't have children? Its magnitude isn't fully realized until you become a parent. It's like you finally and fully comprehend what it means to sacrifice, to be willing to give your life for another. We see noble examples of love in the world (martyrs, soldiers and the best of friends), but the selfless love of a parent? Unquestionable.

There are several covenants in the Bible, all but one (marriage) being between God and man. These are supernatural, extremely spiritual, and when you really think about them, they are blindingly true. God made a covenant with Noah to never again destroy the earth with a flood. And he made another one with the patriarch of the Jewish people, Abraham. "Look up at the heavens and count the stars," He said. "So shall your offspring be" (Genesis 15:5). See how we're right back to the promise of children, as a blessing?

Malachi 2:15 reads, "Has not the LORD made them one? In flesh and spirit they are his. And why one? Because he was seeking godly offspring. So guard yourself in your spirit, and do not break faith with the wife of your youth." The marriage covenant is strong and heavenly blessed. And here it's again coupled with the blessing of children.

"'Love the Lord your God with all your heart and with all your soul and with all your mind,'" Jesus said in Matthew 22:37-40. "This is the first and greatest commandment. And the second is like it: 'Love your neighbor as yourself.' All the Law and the Prophets hang on these two commandments."

Jesus could have stopped with the first command, but he gave a second. And you can't separate these two and call yourself a follower of Christ. Loving God yet despising others is the walk of a hypocrite, as far from God as the religious leaders of Jesus' day who nailed Him to a cross.

So simple, loving God and loving others. And we've learned—in our marriage and in our parenting—how to love. Yet many find it difficult. Why? Because they try to separate the two commands. Those who love God yet form a theology that shoves others to the side are a hideous group of folks, the Pharisees of today. They may claim to be the chosen few, having God all figured out, and packaging their theological dispositions in neat and tidy boxes. But it doesn't take too much of a step back to figure out that they are alone in their faith, and God is not a joyful part of their lives. Because they choose to separate others from God's love, they've removed themselves from Him, too.

On the other end of the spectrum, nonbelievers can care little of the love of God, yet they'd cut off their right arm for their neighbor. We imagine those whom Jesus first called his disciples—commoners and fishermen—as these kinds of folks. They may not have had their relationship with God all figured out, but they apparently knew how to love others. It's interesting how Jesus found Himself more comfortable among this crowd. The disciples—all common folks who chose to share a relationship with Jesus—became steadfast martyrs of the faith, ready and willing to die for their Lord. And it was because they mastered the Greatest Commandment of loving God *and* loving others.

Let's be clear about how we see God and His relationship with us. There is nothing we can do to make Him love us more. He loves us like we love our children. It's a love that is inherent; it's just there, not earned or awarded or created from some behavior. A baby comes and a parent's heart melts. God's love is just like that. He loves us because He made us. He loves you because you are His creation. Case closed. It's that simple.

Don't make it more complicated. If you have a hard time accepting this, it's probably because of some dysfunctional teaching you've received about God. It may have even come from the pulpit; church leaders often miss the importance of the Greatest Commandment. More likely you learned it wrong from your parents who, like you, were young and didn't know how to be loving parents. You are now tasked with bringing children into the world yourself. Are you going to hit the target of love closer to the bull's-eye?

You are a family, and God loves you fully and completely. Why? Because he created you in his own image. He was not asleep when you were made in your mother's womb (Psalm 139:13), and He won't be out to lunch when you conceive a child of your own. He has you on His heart and mind and wants the best for you and your family. God knows you deep down, and He knows you're up for the challenge of family and parenting.

That's good, because it's not like you can walk away from His calling. It'll continue to gnaw at you. His plan for you is custom fit for you and your family. He loves you and will keep pursuing you, no matter how much you try to mess up your relationship with Him. This is love in the deepest sense. You can try to turn on Him and walk away, throw all His blessings in His face, become the most self-centered jerk in the world ... and He will still love you and desire to turn your heart back toward Him.

There are some deep truths in the Greatest Commandment that relate to your family: You can divorce your spouse, abuse your children, ridicule your own parents, even abandon your family altogether, and He will still love you and want the best for you. Most people have a difficult time forgiving others. But God is so incredibly patient with us. He should have zapped us with a bolt of lightning years ago, but His love is covenantal love; it's not possible to excuse. His love never fails, it holds on, it believes in us till the very end. Except that there *is* no end. No matter what we do or don't do, God is still there for us, waiting for us to fully embrace His will for our lives.

Within this truth rest two antithetical choices: a lie and a hope. The lie is that you aren't welcome back. Ever. You failed too much, God will never be able to set you back on track. You, your spouse and your kids are so out of step you'll never dance again. This vicious lie keeps you crippled, distant from God's plan, isolated from His great blessings. Hope is the opposite, an amazing truth: You are one pivotal step away from blissful union with God. You may think you're far away from Him (you're divorced, you had an abortion, you've been abusive, you fill in the blank), but don't be fooled. The conviction to get it right is really God directly behind you. Turn and embrace Him; start loving Him back once again.

Face facts: You have a past of which you're ashamed. We all do, if we're honest with ourselves. It's in our fallen nature to rebel against His love for us. We are destructive, sinful, arrogant and hateful, which is the exact opposite of God. He is the ultimate Creator incapable of these ugly human traits. If you have a perspective of God as a lightning bolt-wielding demigod itching for the chance to zap your slightest sin, you have a dysfunctional image of God, an image likely reflective of a dysfunctional relationship in your past. It's the furthest thing from His love and His truth.

Turning (or returning) to God and growing a relationship with Him is a major step toward understanding the Greatest Commandment. Like parents cheering for the first step of their first child, so God will be cheering you on. You start loving God by allowing Him to love you. It's beautiful and heavenly, a personal relationship you could spend eternity reveling in. And so it is with love in your family, a representation of your love for God and His love for you. You can't separate the two any more than you can separate an atom.

So what happens when you try to split apart God's commands to love? Everything blows up. It's devastating. Pain of separation scar us for life. Many of us who are called to love another child have to deal with these scars of pain. We may have had unloving parents ourselves, or been in abusive relationships in the past. We've witnessed families try to exist without any sort of a relationship with God. We pity them and genuinely feel sorry for them. They are trying their hardest to walk in family unity without grabbing hold of the bond that is right there before them. It's painful. People look at us and see 15 children raised on a single income and think, *How do they do it?* We look at a mom, a dad and two kids without God in their lives, and we wonder the same thing.

Some of them still survive. The covenant of marriage is that strong. We have extended family and old friends who make no bones about it: They do not walk with God. But what they don't realize—and sometimes we find it difficult to accept—is that God is still walking with them. That's how strong the covenant is: God will hold up His end of the bargain even when we won't. His character forbids Him from breaking His word, even when our character practically begs Him to.

It is no mistake that God sees a married couple as one. Not even "tied" together or merely molded together, but one individual unit. It is much like the idea that loving God and loving others are, together, the *one* Greatest Commandment. Matrimony is made in heaven, meant for life.

Two's a Crowd

Like our personal relationship with God, it takes our self-centered humanity to break our marriages up. So many people—sadly, many married couples—do not fully realize the magnificence of the marriage covenant. There is a faulty notion that has plagued many marriages over the years: It's that by fully recognizing and submitting to the covenant of marriage you are somehow surrendering your individuality. Rather than walking in unison as a healthy married couple, a man and a woman will claim that in their marriage, each *individual* is empowered. We've known couples who believe this, and we can't help but think that their relationship is somehow fake, with each one pretending to hold on to a pre-marriage individuality. It's disappointing, really, for by doing so they are sacrificing much of the powerful union of the God-ordained marriage covenant.

Let's return to the seemingly harmless example of money. There's nothing inherently wrong with having two sources of money in your marriage. It may make perfect sense: Dad has a debit card that pays the bills, Mom has one that purchases groceries. Budgeting can be quite helpful, but this isn't how two separate checking accounts typically work in a modern marriage. Instead, these accounts become idols of ownership, "his" money or "her" money. Items purchased become "his" stuff or "her" stuff. Maintenance of said stuff becomes "his" or "her" responsibility.

Advocates for such marriages paste smiles on their faces as they share their clever ideas for dividing the finances most equitably. They get excited over their solutions, and their marriage counselors are so proud of them for fairly dividing up the family income and expenses. They move forward confidently with tidy budgets and responsible divisions, each adding to the family assets with more "his" and "her" stuff. These marriages are full of fairness and equality, a neat house of cards built together.

Until the car breaks down. These advocates for equal separation in a marriage may easily split such an expense, but what if the breakdown is because of the husband's failure to get the oil changed? Should it then not be his responsibility? Or the wife overspends on groceries that month, is the husband expected to throw in his money? What started out as a harmless budgeting solution—one that empowered individuality and kept husband and wife autonomous and supposedly strong—quickly becomes a wedge in the marriage.

Or maybe somebody gets sick. If the husband is sick, he can't work and the wife may need to step up and work outside the home. If the wife is sick, the husband must do both jobs of breadwinner and housekeeper. For the marriage that is already one, this is not too much to ask. We're married "in sickness and in health," after all, and it's the loving thing to do. For the marriage of *equality*, though, the temptation to bolt from the imbalance becomes great, and the desire to run from responsibility seems a valid option. The house of cards falls down, leaving a mess for one spouse to pick up. Such marriages seldom hold on to their equality to the end.

Marriages that last often dump the idea of "two equal entities." Yet the separate-but-equal mentality still lingers for many. And, again, money seems to be the perfect example. Husbands resent wives for racking up credit card bills on household items, and wives rag on their husbands for big-ticket hunting items. So goes the stereotypical married couple. "We share our money and have only one bank account," they boast, yet they still cling to their individual items—household or hunting gear—and build resentment toward one another for hoarding.

A husband and wife are in the boat together—rowing in different directions. The result? They spin in a circle, in the middle of a lake, going nowhere fast. What happened? The two were rowing in unison at first. But she started to become frustrated with him for not rowing like a man, and he grew frustrated with her for not being very helpful. They popped out a child or two and started disagreeing over parenting and schooling and discipline. Their rowing became dizzying, and the temptation to jump ship grew stronger every day.

My solution (Wendy's) is for this lady in the boat to take a good hard look at her husband and make a decision: Let him lead or continue to let this ship sink. Not much of a choice, I know, but are you in this for life or aren't you? Are you in this for the good of your family or for yourself? You probably should have let him take the oars right from the get-go, but better late than never.

Wait, before you expose your claws, let me explain. God's idea and perfect plan is for one person to lead. The boat needs a captain. Your role as captain's mate is not less than his. Different, yet let him do the rowing. Let him lead, and you hang on and enjoy the ride. Ask him where he's going and how you can help him get there. You will find that this is the most excellent and exciting way to fuel your marriage. It is the most loving thing a wife can do for her husband.

My solution (Chris') is to take those oars seriously. You may have to stop rowing for a while to truly engage with your wife, consider her concerns and her navigation. Women have an innate depth about them, so much deeper than guys, an intuition that can help direct the ship of your family in ways you would never fathom. This depth is what attracted you to her in the first place. Seek her opinion, explore her heart. She wants you to lead, but she also wants to help. Don't disregard her ideas, become threatened by them or treat her like a child. Chances are she's right much more than she's wrong. This is how you should love her.

These are marriages that work as one. Matrimony is a covenant, much more than equal partners. Such marriages are able to conquer any obstacle in their way. They are able to stand against enemies at the gate and move mountains. There is no room for wedges, no slight crack of separation that allows the worm of lies to start separating. These marriages are solid, built to last, and perfect for loving more children.

Solution for Contention

Since both of us have walked through this problem with money, we've come up with some fantastic solutions. They are much more valuable than the bean-counting fantasy of "separate but equal." Our solutions attempt to truly merge a couple into one cohesive, synchronized marriage that allows them to walk the path God has for them. Ultimately, the oneness of your marriage should be freeing and empowering, not confining or limiting.

Here's one solution: Put off contention and go with agreement. Two years ago, we both decided it was time to sell our RV.[22] We did, and the money we made financed the start of a remodeling of our kitchen. New counters, new cabinets, new floors, new stove— it looks great. We both agreed that this was a good use of the money we made from the sale, so we went with it. We were in total unison on the decision ... but all decisions lead to details that are not foreseeable.

Like most projects, it cost more than we had available. Disagreement ultimately surfaced. Our old ugly refrigerator—with its cracked drawers and broken ice maker—remained. I (Wendy) wanted a new one, Chris said the old one works fine. And so the contention started.

Instead of a new refrigerator, Chris believed a four-wheeler ATV would be much more practical. All the kids are on his side, too. Not only would it be a lot of fun, it would be helpful during hunting and doing chores around our 6 acre property. I saw nothing but turmoil in maintaining such an expensive and unsafe machine. A refrigerator made much more sense to me.

And so this contention sits. It doesn't fester, it just sits. We aren't buying a refrigerator and we're not buying an ATV. We're quite content with the way things are and since we didn't come to a financial agreement, we are letting it be.

But do you see how this could be a wedge in our marriage? I had my own credit card, so what would stop me from ordering the new one in spite of what Chris thought? Chris, too, could have scrounged up enough money to buy that ATV. If either of us did this, though, we'd obviously be moving in anything but a loving, unified direction. Neither of us would be looking out for the other's interests. Neither would be considerate of the other. We'd be hypocrite dancers stepping on each other's toes with resentment and distrust.

Writing this book, we still have the old fridge ... and no ATV. The funny thing is, though, we're both fine with it. We share this story with other couples, and they sometimes pick sides, as if we're asking them to. "Why doesn't Chris just buy Wendy the darn fridge; that's much more practical than an ATV." "Who wears the pants in the house, Chris? Get the darn ATV and let's go huntin'!" It's so easy to identify with our plight, but we laugh at it and are totally fine with letting the days roll on without allowing it fester. It's not like the old fridge isn't doing its job, and it's not like we aren't able to get work done without an ATV. We love each other too much to let this issue become a dividing one. Funnier yet, Chris knows I would be fine if he went out and bought an ATV, but such a move isn't even on his mind. He wants to please me, and I want to please him. The conflict becomes a non-issue, and our marriage dance continues.

Unstoppable

What a miraculous covenant marriage is! There is no stronger bond made between man and woman. It's safe to say that God's vow to mankind and His view of our vows in marriage are the most important contracts that can be created. God is on your side, He wants your marriage to succeed, He wants your family to grow in love and, perhaps, children.

That's comforting to note, isn't it? The God of the universe is in it for *you*. Satan—the chump—is out to destroy you, but you wield the power of heaven itself to thwart his evil ways. Don't underestimate the power of your marriage, and don't underestimate the Adversary's attempts to bring it down. At the first thought of its weakness, stomp it out like the ugly snake it is. Make a habit of it. Don't think your family is frivolous or easy to discard. The moment a negative thought of your spouse enters your head, nail it to the wall where it belongs. Shout it out, if you have to, like Jesus did: "Get behind me, Satan!" (Matthew 16:23, Mark 8:33). Then press on.

When that habit is made, you can face the cruel world together, arm in arm, ready to take on whatever it has to dish out. The difficult lesson of overcoming your own individuality, submitting to your spouse and embracing the plan God has for your family—it's now behind you. You can *love another child* with open arms. No manipulation, no infighting, no resentment or regret.

Such a family is not easily broken. It's nearly unstoppable. You and your spouse are ready to build a heritage of love.

8 - Loving Your Children

"Jesus not only loved the children but went further, stipulating a condition that applied to everybody: It is necessary to become like a child to enter the kingdom of heaven. The phrase 'like a child' means here to be innocent, simple, open, genuine and good."—Mother Teresa

You may think you have God all figured out, but if you feel a lack of love for your neighbor (or spouse or child or relative), something is out of sync. You're missing something, and like a good student of a logic puzzle, you've got to figure it out. Parents of children seem to never be at a loss of opportunities to practice this.

We've addressed the fear that your marriage may fall apart, and we hope that by facing that fear your marriage starts a spiral up rather than the more common spiral down. Now, let's go back to that embedded fear you have for having children. The same kind of spiral can happen with your children.

When pressed, most parents will vehemently say they love their children. Who wouldn't? It is when they are alone with their closest confidants that they open up and are more truthful. There are those children who get under our skin. We have 15 children, so we have a lot of personalities to deal with. Loving some has been more difficult than others, but never impossible. Unfortunately, many (most?) parents allow resentment *(unlove?)* to fester in their relationship with one or two children—the tougher children—and the results are devastating to the family. Take this example:

"I have tried and tried to get Tommy to do his chores. He is so lazy. I have never said that to his face, I've tried to encourage him, punish him, ground him, whatever ... but he still takes three hours to do dishes when it's supposed to be time for school. All his siblings are frustrated with him, so I'm not the only one. I have pleaded with him to get moving, but he still slides along like a snail. Then he'll lie to me, pretend to be sick, get angry and fight with his siblings. He'll cry and cry, and he's nearly a teenager! I don't know if there's anything else I can do to get him to change. I'm considering sending him to boarding school, because I just can't take it any longer."

Do you have a child like Tommy? Tommy has trouble doing his chores and he slows the entire day up. In a family our size we have quite a few Tommys! Maybe it's not chores: It could be homework, getting along with siblings, back talking, etc.

How do you love a Tommy? We may have to come to terms with the fact that Tommy isn't going to be the fast cleaner his older or younger siblings are. And this begs the question: What about the dishes? Are we supposed to feed Tommy's laziness?

We have a solution, and, as with marriage, it has everything to do with love. For us, the Twelve Step Process prayer works miracles. It's called the Serenity Prayer, and it is prayed by millions of Alcoholics Anonymous members around the world. It's a beautiful prayer by Dr. Reinhold Niebuhr:

God, grant me the serenity
To accept the things I cannot change;
Courage to change the things I can;
And wisdom to know the difference.

This is a most profound way to show our love to our children. Like with our spouses, we should become students of them. Know them. Find the things that are easy to love and help them grow. There are those things we must discipline, but the example above is sorely in error. This parent has shut off any positive aspect of Tommy, as well as any potential solution.

But we see a lot of hope in this situation. And it doesn't start with Tommy. Those points of exasperation need to be analyzed carefully, and let us as parents pray for the wisdom to work with Tommy. Here are three ways to start turning this problem around, all three of them involving aspects of love.

1. "Love is not easily angered" (1 Corinthians 13:5).

Refuse to get angry over the problem. Find ways to overcome the anger and replace it with servitude, humor and time-outs (for yourself!). If a child's behavior leads you to anger or frustration, you have *got* to figure out the problem. Justifying your anger or blaming it on your child is submitting to the lies of hate that will undermine your relationship with him.

This is a most common failure for young parents. We failed in this when we were younger. We were stricter with our first children, and we would quickly grow weary and expect much more conformity than we do now. Our parenting was focused more on conformity than on love, on frustration rather than grace.

This is typical. The first children in any family go through the ringer with Mom and Dad. By the time the last child moves through, Mom and Dad are far more easygoing and not nearly as uptight. In fact, it's not uncommon for older children to envy how relaxed their parents are with the younger children. Today we are grandparents, we're expecting more children of our own, and we are extremely laid back. Trust us, the laid back way is the better way to go.

There are times of anger (note the adverb "easily" in the verse), but more often than not they are weak moments in our parenting. Imagine what you sound like to a stranger outside your front door. Are your reactions to your child's behavior commendable or shocking? Would you be embarrassed if you had a video camera capture your tone? The second anger rises in you, check yourself. Anger is one of the Enemy's favorite tools to worm his way in and start driving a wedge between you and your child. Like in your marriage, pause, reflect and put the anger behind you. Then move on to handle the situation with grace and love.

There will be times that frustration with our little Tommys get the best of us. When this is a consistent habit, though, parents should try hard to get it corrected. This takes prayer, surrendering your temper to the Cross, and perhaps getting some outside help from a pastor or counselor. We know this can be a humiliating admission for a parent, but there is little more damaging than a hot temper. Parents who are "easily angered" are removing love from their relationship with their child. Take as much to God as you can, one step at a time, a little bit more at a time.

Bringing your frustrations "to the Cross" may be a new concept for you. This can be one of the most spiritual aspects to your parenting. Your children will do irrational, unloving, silly, disobedient things. Count on it. "Folly is bound up in the heart of a child," reads Proverbs 22:15. If such folly drives you to poor behavior, you need to first get a hold of yourself. It may not be easy at first, but Christ is willing to accept your admissions of failure. If all you can do is bring 10 percent, bring 10 percent to Him and pray for resolution. God is always ready for you to surrender your problems to Him. He is your heavenly Father.

Here's a typical response: "You don't *know* how bad I have it." But that's the same justification as the dissatisfied housewife or disrespected husband gives. This parent keeps track of the sins of the child and lets bitterness fester—which is our next point.

2. "Love keeps no record of wrongs" (1 Corinthians 13:5).

We know, it may seem like Tommy will never move fast, but you know what? That may be OK. Stop nagging him to move fast. Instead, begin studying him to figure out what makes him tick. Perhaps he's an eccentric type, or an artist, or a creative genius. Consider also that this may be a hormonal change; his emotions may be more physiological than you realize. You need to love him and find the best in him, rather than shame him into proper behavior. Shaming him will never lead to the behavior you want.

So rather than shame, try encouragement. When a child is having a difficult time with a certain behavior (like Tommy with the dishes) keeping track of his performance is often counterproductive. Encouragement—like love—does not keep track of negative performance, but is like a cheering section. We all need a cheering section sometimes, and parents can be some of the best cheerleaders.

Parents can also be some of the best coaches. Good coaches keep track of performance, but not to belittle or condemn their players. We are big believers in *practicing* proper behavior, role-playing what we expect from our children. We often catch ourselves growing frustrated with our children for things *we think* they should know. Coming alongside them and training them like a coach would train his players—perhaps washing the dishes with little Tommy—gets better (never perfect, but better) performance.

Remember, you will *not* get perfect behavior out of your children. If you set this as an expectation, you will be disappointed. In fact, you'll get extremely frustrated and you'll likely exasperate them. "Fathers, do not exasperate your children," Ephesians reminds us. "Instead, bring them up in the training and instruction of the Lord." Your children need your coaching, and they can always use a cheering section, but if you rack up their failures and shortcomings, and use them to manipulate their behavior, you will not succeed in getting anything out of your child.

Consider this for a moment: Does the Lord unleash His anger every time *you* step out of line? Does he keep a record of all the misery you brought upon His family every time you fail? No, He doesn't. His training is consistent and firm, but always loving. This is the loving way to react to the sins of our children. Once dealt with, forget it. "As far as the east is from the west, so far has he removed our transgressions from us" (Psalm 103:12). Return to loving your child, smiles, hugs and pats on the shoulder.

"But he does this over and over and over again!" you may say, with self-righteous anger building up in you. Remember, we have 15 children, and a few of them had real doozies for behavior problems. We doubt your kids' behavior would faze us. Your anger and record of wrongs never do the behavior-changing you think. At its core, these shortcomings fail to do much of anything other than frustrate everyone in the family. Our last point explains.

3. "If I speak in the tongues of men and of angels, but have not love, I am only a resounding gong or a clanging cymbal" (1 Corinthians 13:1).

This is how Tommy views our insistence to change his behavior, when that insistence is born of annoyance, ridicule or anger. Ever get the glassy-eyed stare back, as if what you're saying is going in one ear and out the other? Chances are good that your rebuke is out of anger, you're rattling off a litany of history, and you sound like a clanging cymbal. Your child has turned you off in his mind, and the wedge of separation has started.

Tame your tongue. It can be a whip to your child's heart. It isn't that your words aren't getting through; your kids just can't take the nagging any longer. You are an unloving gong that had numbed their ears. This verse—the one that kicks off 1 Corinthians 13's "love verses," some of which were likely recited at your wedding—says that it doesn't matter how holy your other speech is. If you don't have love, your words are mere noise. Damaging, to say the least.

Just as it is easier to get compliance out of little children, it is easier to love them. This is so true, so easy when you think about it. If you struggle with growing upset with a particular child—you know, the one you think of when reading this chapter!—flick a switch in your mind. Read the rest of 1 Corinthians 13 and vow to react in such ways. Be patient, kind, protecting, trusting, hoping, persevering—all of it. If your child is young, you'll be quite surprised at how quickly his heart will turn back to you.

If your child is older—a teenager or even an adult—it'll take more time. If you have a history of clanging-cymbal outbursts, the walls of disparity are likely pretty thick. Perhaps that whip of the tongue has experienced a backlash, and your teen has grown up enough and is articulate enough to dish it back at you. Don't give up. You may need to have a heart-to-heart, asking for genuine forgiveness for your lack of love as a parent. There's no shame in seeking forgiveness from your child.

Man up, parents. You're the grown-ups here. Don't let *unlove* fester in your home. In all your parenting, reach first for love—before any other kind of correction. You will seldom go wrong. "Love never fails" (verse 8). This is how your children will remember you and how your heritage will be built: with love. Even faith and hope fall short of the impact your love will have on your family. "The greatest of these is love" (verse 13).

The Student Is You

Back to that idea about being a student of your children. It seems kind of backwards, doesn't it? Especially if you are a homeschool family like ours. We don't mean you necessarily learn anything from your children (though you will in more ways than you can imagine). We mean you should study your children, know their ins and outs, figure out what makes them tick. Doing so is what every loving parent should do. Your children, we're sure, are incredible people, and if you think otherwise, you're missing something big. So let's explore some practical ways to do that.

Recognize that your child may be caught in a very natural stage of development. Funny how we learn so much about developmental psychology in college, yet we throw it all out the window when we become parents. We've raised children all the way through to adulthood, so we're able to see what are stages and what aren't. What we would give to have been able to posses this insight when we were younger!

How can you? Here's how: Whatever leads your child to frustration, pause and analyze. We believe this is what Ephesians 6:4 means when it says, "Do not exasperate your children." When you are, realize that something isn't right and you need to figure it out. More often than not, it's a stage in development.

We were reflecting on this a few days before our little Zechariah turned 1. He's having trouble communicating his wishes while in the high chair. He screams—ear-piercing screams—that are annoying. We recalled earlier years in our parenting where we would react with frustration first, or sharply scold our kids for screaming, taking quick disciplinary action as if the baby was defying his parents. We still say "no" and urge Zech to not scream, but we don't go down the frustrating path of discipline. Why not? Because it's a stage, one that will pass in a few short months, and he'll learn signs and how to talk soon enough.

Another practical way to handle problems: Remind your children of your love for them. It's never good to assume that they know this. Verbally affirm your love for them while you're doing laundry, educating, making sacrifices, and so on. Shouldn't your children *know* you're doing all this out of love for them? But the truth is, they don't always know.

Your love for your children rubs off on them, and they'll start treating one another with love, too. One of our Tommys was very much annoying his sister, Lydia, who is our best cleaner-upper. Give her a chore and *snap* it's done. She was building up a heart of anger and resentment toward her brother. While we were working with her brother on this problem, she started to become angry with us for "letting" him be lazy. The spiral *down* was, for a while, vicious. But then it started to move *up*. Why? Because this was an opportunity to teach her to love her brother even though he wasn't wired like her. There were some tense moments in the house, but they were filled with opportunities to learn how to love.

Lydia recently wrote a speech for a competition about sibling rivalry, and she referred back to this relationship in it. It's a beautiful example of how she learned to forgive her brother, see his greatest strength, and love him. Here's the section of her oratory:

> Why don't I like my brother or sister? I don't know, he just ... just ... he just bugs me! My younger siblings are plain-old annoying, and my older siblings are Miss Know-It-Alls. [But] irritations are opportunities for us to learn and grow, to enhance the relationship at hand, to learn to love each other.

Being able to focus on what's good about a sibling helped me in my relationship with my younger brother, Isaiah. See, he has a habit for taking *forever* to do the dishes. He's only a couple years younger than me, so there was no excuse for his slowness other than *laziness*. This part of his personality was small but was big to me a couple years ago. I was resolved: Isaiah should be faster! How fast? Why, as fast as me, of course. I grew so angry when trying to change him that our relationship was just miserable. There were times when I wished he wasn't my brother at all. Sad, isn't it?

At first, I thought it would be impossible. Forgiving him and trying to look at his good side? Come on, the dishes were taking forever! But I gave it a try. I started to look at his good side. I also started to "pretend" to ignore his slowness. It wasn't easy at first, but over time I found my attitude begin to change. You know, Isaiah is the most easygoing agreeable kind of guy. I focused on that. I started to grow more patient with him about his chores. In fact, I started to like him once again, more and more as time went on.

Now, Isaiah still takes forever to do the dishes, but I'm refusing to allow that to get on my nerves. Isaiah is a very special guy.

Isn't that great? We are so proud of Lydia for making it through that tough time. And we're proud of Isaiah, too. He had to learn how important others saw his work in sharing the tasks around the house. It was a growing opportunity for both of them. Their attempts to change each other was leading nowhere, but their love didn't fail.

If you have more than one child, you will naturally compare one with the other. We have 15. Strange as it may sound, God shows us how to love each one of them. Really, though, when you think about it, it's not strange at all. Love multiplies, it knows no bounds, and when we ask God for wisdom on love, He is faithful to give it to us. Each one of our children comes with his or her individual challenges, and addressing each challenge with love (as opposed to ridicule, shame, scorn, manipulation, etc.) shows us over and over again how rewarding the Greatest Commandment is.

We love homeschooling. It is an adventure to which we believe God is calling more and more parents. Even after nearly 20 years of homeschooling, every year brings new and exciting things to our family. We don't want to put a damper on this excitement at all, but let's burst a bubble that may be in your heart: *Homeschooling will not bring purity to your family.*

Remember what we said earlier, and what the principles of 1 Corinthians 13 supports: Anything placed in front of love is futile—homeschooling included. There are a lot of myths flying around in the heads of dedicated parents ready to begin braving home-based education. Their great expectations include raising perfect children, keeping them from sin, delivering them from evil, and on the wish list goes. We can almost hear the angels saying, "Foolish mortals."

Seriously, such nonsense creates ugly homes. Parents like these place a dysfunctional expectation on their children. Failure to instill a foundation of love in these homeschools (or any home, no matter the choice of education) is failure to build a home at all. When homes have a deficit of love, it is common to see the very things we've wished away come back to haunt us. Toddlers have tantrums, children fight with one another, teens flirt with rebellion, and so on. Something needs to fill the void of love, and it's usually something undesirable.

If you think you have the most difficult child on the planet, think again. Check that heart of yours first before you allow those thoughts to fester. Chances are good that you're the one exasperating your child, and you should stop it. Stop making excuses for *his* or *her* bad behavior, become a student of your children, and figure out what you need to do to love them through it. This kind of love will build a family heritage that will be fondly remembered when your children are old.

Learn to Love

Our first book, *Love in the House*, offers up creative ideas to seek compliance from your children. We tried very hard to give practical tools for high-strung parents. For the most part, we think we succeeded. We get to the end of our rope just like any parent, but we've learned over the years how to handle it with love. I (Wendy) wrote the following, and it exemplifies a lot of what we're saying. It's worth repeating here:

We have not been perfect parents any more than our children have been perfect kids. The longer we parent and the more children we have, the more we are convinced that loving one another is the most important thing we need to master in life. Some argue that having so many children weakens our ability to love them all, but we disagree. There is a multiplying phenomenon that occurs in large families where there is strength in numbers and a compounding of love.

As already mentioned, I came from a broken family. However, I never used this as an excuse for making poor choices as a parent myself. We all have choices to make, and choosing to love your children is the greatest of all choices. Failing to consciously make the choice to love can, unfortunately, hinder your relationship with your children.

A couple years ago I began to view my children in a unique way. I envisioned them with a sign around their neck that read, "I don't know that you love me." This is the truth: they don't know for sure. It is very easy for parents to take for granted that their children know their love for them. We do dishes, fold laundry, tuck them in at night, and work our tails off for them; naturally, we *assume* they know our love for them, but they don't. My parenting changed for the better when I recognized that I needed to verbally show my love for my children.

I have shown this in both subtle and direct ways. Standing in the kitchen making dinner, I'll blurt out, "Cynthia, I want you to know that I really, really love you." When my 5-year-old brings me a book to read to her, I'll say, "Hannah, if I didn't have a Hannah just like you, I would *want* a Hannah just like you." I say things like this constantly. As I say these words of affirmation of my love for them, I transform my thinking, I believe them to be true, and my children grow to believe the same.

I also see my kids—especially when they grow into teenagers—each with an emotional cup. He or she brings me the cup daily as if to say, "Please fill my cup today, Mom." This is shown by bringing a book to read, playing a game, help with schoolwork, etc. If I don't pour my love into the cup, the child will eventually turn away and seek other avenues for the love for which they hope. Parents should not give up filling their children's cups with love.

So far in this book we have attempted to encourage you to allow God to bless your family life. Overcoming fears, being creative, embracing freedom, practicing proper behavior, developing relationships—these are all good and worthy objectives parents should have. The practical applications in this book all boil down to one main objective, a most important objective. This is *love*, a virtue too often underrated in busy families. We are guilty of missing the mark on loving relationships in the past. Through our trials—which we share in the remaining chapters—we have come to the firm conclusion that *love in the house* is the greatest of goals.

We won't go into the conflict we had with our oldest child here. (Read about that in our previous book.) Suffice it to say it was a heartbreaking story that unfolded deep lessons about loving our children first and foremost. Our point here is this: Do not make the mistake of thinking that your parenting should wield something greater than love. There is nothing, and every attempt at something greater is inevitably regretted. Embrace it. Make a habit of it. Years from now, when your house is full of children and overflowing with loving relationships, you will not carry regret on your heart. You will have *love in the house*.

---

9 - Check Out or Stand In

"I've never heard a dying soul / Wish that he had taken more time on his portfolio / I swear, I've never heard a mama say / 'Should've never had that baby' as a doctor holds her newborn on display." —dcTalk, "Wanna Be Loved"

A life with 15 children has its peculiarities, like finding the best deal in town on eggs ... and then frequenting that store often. For us, it is our local Walmart, and the best deal is purchasing the 18-count cartons. We go through about two dozen eggs a day, so it's not uncommon for one of us to pull our carts up to the checkout line with about 20 packages. This morning there was a new checkout lady that I (Wendy) had never seen before.

"What on earth are you using all these eggs for?" she asked me. She was in her 20s, and judging from the ring on her finger, was married.

"We eat them," I answered. "We have eggs for breakfast almost every morning."

Now she was *really* curious. "How big is your family?" she asked, her eyes widening.

"We have 13 children at home."

The scanner stopped beeping. The checkout lady froze, mouth ajar. "Did you say *thirteen?*"

I nodded and smiled, sort of curious myself as to how she would respond from there. I've gotten all sorts of responses over the years, folks nearly falling over in awe or even flat-out disbelieving, as if I was a compulsive liar. This Walmart associate's response was one of the most common.

"How do you do it?" And not waiting for a response, she related me to her own experience as a mother. "I go crazy with just my two! *Thirteen!* I'd go crazy."

"No you wouldn't," I countered. "You could love another child."

There was another pause. A reflective pause.

If I could freeze time and psychoanalyze this young lady's current life, it would be so predictable, so cookie-cutter similar to so many young women today. She hadn't always been a checkout lady at Walmart. She fell in love at a young age, and she and her husband had stars in their eyes. They had so much optimism for their future. They started a family—one, then two children—and life's pressures weighed in. Mortgage, day care, car seat laws, flippant comments from childless friends or in-laws. Birth control and a second job seemed so much easier, the natural way to go.

This mother, like most ladies in their 20s, wants to have and hold another baby, but every single cultural persuasion pushes against her. She's been told that having a third child is overpopulating the earth and is harmful to the environment. Her mentors tell her likewise—her parents, her closest friends and her neighbors. Some would verbally ostracize her for even thinking of having another child. Her husband would question the responsibility of such a move. Another child would be another mouth to feed and more financial burden to the family, especially the likely loss of the extra income brought in by working at Walmart. Another child brings bondage, exhaustion, dirty diapers, sleepless nights, responsibility, and on and on the list goes.

The checkout mom would have thought I was psychic. But checkout lines at every shopping center in the country are run by moms living the exact same life.

She shrugged, chuckled uncomfortably and said, "I don't think so." She continued to scan the cartons of eggs.

On the way home I pondered her response. Is she really thinking through her decisions? She doesn't "think" she could have another child. But where do her thoughts come from? What's persuaded her to think so? Why has she suppressed her heartfelt desire to have another child, and in exchange for what? Is working the checkout at Walmart really what she wanted for her and her family when she fell in love and married her husband?

The Path Back to the Fruitful Life

At the risk of using clichés, this mother has continued down the well-trod path. It's easy, it's what everyone else is doing, little thought needs to come into it. Robert Frost's classic poem "The Road Not Taken" ends like this:

> I shall be telling this with a sigh
> Somewhere ages and ages hence:
> Two roads diverged in a wood, and I—
> I took the one less traveled by,
> And that has made all the difference.

And what a difference this life has been, this life of bearing children and cultivating a house of love to raise them in. Why would any parent desire another path? Yet there remains a doubt in many of our minds that the less traveled path really does yield more joy than the more traveled one. We want to erase that doubt.

This checkout mom, like so many young women today, chose the well-traveled path. Her choices likely started with simple ones, easy ones that seemed like no big deal—like ordering a pizza instead of cooking dinner herself. But multiply that one little decision by even 20, and the bills stack up, and a young family needs a second income to afford all the "stand-ins."

A stand-in comes to your home and cleans. It's easy to pay that bill, it seems. Certainly it's easier than cleaning yourself. Local schools and even homeschool co-ops stand in to educate your children. How hard is it to enroll Jimmy and Janie and drop them off? Hey, why not carpool with other moms or take advantage of the school bus routes? We need that extra job to pay for our stand-ins, and day care is so convenient. Six weeks after another child you can be back at work.

Funny how we can never find a stand-in for our jobs, though. Wouldn't it be convenient to hire a replacement to go to work for you? That's where the stand-ins stop. The money needed for all the stand-ins must come from someplace, and that place is work, even if work is scanning egg cartons at the grocery store.

Blast back to reality, parents. All these stand-ins have done nothing but rack up bills and pull you away from the loving family you could have. It's nearly laughable that some people look at our life and think *we're* the crazy ones. To us, the oft-walked path of dual incomes, day care, public school, frozen dinners, fashionable wardrobes, sinking mortgages, car payments, etc., seems the crazier, more anxiety-filled choice.

I (Wendy) couldn't help but overhear one mom talking with another mom at the gym recently. She was talking about picking up her daughter after kindergarten. (I assumed her daughter was at kindergarten that morning.) Apparently, her daughter had wet shoes and was wearing someone else's clothes. No note, no nothing, just a wet daughter—in February—in different clothes than what she put on that morning. Like any mom, she marched back into the school demanding an explanation. Her daughter got wet at recess, she was told, and the school had her find dry clothes in the lost-and-found bin. The staff apologized for not calling, for the school being understaffed that day, for not noticing the wet shoes, and on the excuses went.

We know, stories of the deficiencies of public school are a dime a dozen. And this one's not even one of the worst. Metal detectors, suspensions handed out for bringing butter knives to lunch, putting prophylactics on bananas in 6th grade—we've all heard about such things. What choices does this mom have? She could accept the school's excuses. She could start volunteering in the school. She could transfer to a private school. Or she could take her daughter out of school altogether. She chose the first option. I heard her explain to her friend, "I'm glad I didn't make a fool of myself in the office by overreacting."

Yes, this mother at the gym had many choices, just like the clerk at Walmart. She'd get a thumbs-up from the Jeubs and millions of other homeschool parents if she pulled the plug on state-run, taxpayer-funded education for her family. We would smile on her like we smile on the young couple who overcome their fear and have their first child. She'd be on her way to discovering the great joy and reward that comes with home education.

Even if she didn't jump right into the homeschool pool, she could begin to apply some parent-directed principles. Most parents who end up homeschooling do start out small. I (Chris) have my teaching degree and had taught in the public schools in the '90s, so our decision to homeschool was a gradual, well-researched one. We were right there with that mother 20 years prior, wrestling with that parental tug at our hearts, wondering if we should own our children's educational development in the same way that we owned their spiritual development.

Parents may—and should—push back against cultural expectations that would harm their children. No one should apologize for being upset with neglectful schools, and parents who feel they have no choice but to pull their children out of public school should be applauded for fighting to find a better way.

It's easy to go with the flow, but we say swim upstream for the betterment of your children. Millions of parents make financial sacrifices to choose alternative education (Christian schools, for example) while still paying their taxes to their local public schools. That's not fair, but it just might be the best money they've ever spent. Some states actually encourage alternative education with school choice policies, but not nearly enough.

We are so pleased that homeschooling has become so much more accepted as one of those alternatives. It's easier to get started now than it ever has been. Though state laws vary, most do not require enrollment until the first grade or 7 years old. Many parents "give it a try" at these early ages and, lo and behold, they discover the joys of parenting *and educating* their very own children. A kindergartner is incredibly easy to educate; parents teach the ABC's and how to tie a shoe at this age; trigonometry comes much later. What these parents soon discover is that home education—usually without fail—produces much better results than sending kids off to the local, more convenient, public school.

I (Wendy) have a house of teens and a self-employed husband, so taking off for an hour workout at the gym is easy for me. I wouldn't be able to do that otherwise, and I didn't back when all my children were small. Life happens, and my priority has always been to mother my children, so the cultural expectations would always get knocked off as my husband and I organized our family life.

It doesn't take too much nowadays to convince people of the benefits of alternative education. Situations like this mother's are usually the first step to questioning the success of the local public school. On a more personal level, the conflict often has to do with a surrender of responsibility. A mother is expected to surrender her children to the school system, and that expectation goes largely unchallenged.

Clearly we love home education! And the decision to do so is one we encourage of parents. But that's not really our point here. Our point is this: Parents often *check out* when they let others *stand in*.

We were right there with that mother 20 years ago. We justified the stand-in school despite the tug in our hearts to take more responsibility ourselves. We did what we could: We volunteered often, sat in with other parents at parent-teacher meetings and did our best to communicate with the teachers. Many of them had huge hearts of gold; some were excellent educators. However, we knew even then that no matter how well-intentioned they were, they would never love our children as much as we did.

We're sure you know parents who are disconnected from those kinds of feelings, out of touch totally with their children. They aren't happy parents. A dad may live to go out with his buddies rather than play catch with his son. A mom may be closer to her Facebook friends than her own daughter. We see family situations like this and we want to shake the moms and dads and say, "Don't you realize that these days to connect with your children are slipping away?"

Perhaps that's you. If so, bringing another child into your checked-out family would be meaningless. That sounds harsh, we know. It's difficult to share this opinion in writing because it so quickly sounds judgmental. And we don't want you to think we don't empathize or understand. We know it's tough—swimming against the current always is. Our hearts go out to parents who feel they have little choice but to "go with the flow" and have everyone else in life stand in for their parenting.

"You Have Everything"

One of our favorite parties every year is our homeschool group's Christmas party, a time when perhaps 40 or so couples gather to celebrate the season. We typically have it at somebody else's home— one of the big 10,000-square-foot homes that a few of the families are blessed with—but last year we decided to host the party in our 2,400-square-foot modular. One mother who was new to our group spoke fondly of our family, saying she had heard about "that huge family in Monument," and was grateful to finally meet us. She has five children (no small feat nowadays), and she and I got wrapped up in a fun conversation. Our talk bounced from home education to recipes to shopping the deals—all those things moms like us find interesting.

The vulnerable words leapt from her throat, with hesitation, as if she was not sure she should say them, but did anyway: "I wish we didn't stop at five." Tears started to fill her eyes. She was comparing her life with mine (not something I necessarily feel comfortable with), and her regret was obvious. She and her husband cut the line of blessing several years prior, not for any physical or financial reason or much thought at all. They just did. They went with the flow. "You have everything," she said.

What could I say or do other than give her a big hug? She's right, I do have everything. I may not have the financial blessing, but I have the infrastructure I need: big van, infant car seat, high chair and crib. I'm already home full-time, why not have another baby? What greater desire is there than living a life without regret? At the time this mother made her observation, the house was in order, the children were busy downstairs with projects, and we adults were having a ball sharing Christmas cookies and gifts. We look our best at Christmas parties. But even so, our moments of struggles (a messy house, crunched schedules, tight finances) don't hinder the blessed life. We follow God, He blesses us. It's simple, and we have no regrets.

How common it is for parents to live with the regret of cutting off their heritage. This life goes by so quickly, and what we set our mind to eventually defines us. We think we're doing our children a favor by seeking material blessings and securing that second job to finance it, or hiring the stand-in to accommodate it, but we're really not. We tend to think we're hopeless, throwing all sorts of excuses in our way, thinking we aren't able to do what God has placed on our hearts.

This is key. It is unbelief to think that you aren't able to walk the path that God asks you to walk. I have everything, but so does every Christian! Following Christ with the confidence that He will provide for your every need is the epitome of the Lord's Prayer. Our beautiful Christian faith is one of a personal relationship with God, like a Father invested in the success of His children, and He wants us to live the blessed life to the fullest.

No matter what your situation, you can place your hope in this personal relationship. What He lays on your heart, do. Don't look for alternatives or counterfeits, just do what He is calling you to do. There's no situation bleak enough to substitute for the simple faith God calls you to exercise. You can check out or check in, get a stand-in or stand up yourself. No matter how hopeless you think you are, hope in Jesus Christ trumps *everything*. My personal testimony speaks to this:

When I was little, I spent most of my time at my neighbor's home. My father walked out on the family, and my mom had to work full time to provide for my five siblings and me. I remember pockets of love in my childhood, but seldom what my heart desired. Preschool was a horrid place where a teacher's aide slapped a yard stick over our heads for refusing to take the required nap. Because I complained so much to my mom, she let me stay with our neighbor, and they were, thankfully, open to helping a single mom.

Sound hopeless? You bet it does. My mom didn't have the choices of most parents in her day. Single parents seldom do. So our message isn't a condemnation of those who struggle; our message is all about creativity, adapting to the challenges of life, moving against popular sentiment. My mom did the best thing she could: She took me out of preschool. And she showed me that even though her choices were limited, she still *had* choices, and some of the ones she made were very good.

So don't think, "The Jeubs don't understand our predicament!" Chances are good that your situation is not nearly as bad as you've made it out to be. You have everything you need to love another child. You always have.

Resist Conformity

It's too easy today to miss the marrow of life that is parenting. Growing up in the '70s and '80s, homeschooling wasn't even an option to consider; those who homeschooled back then are today considered the pioneers of the movement, and sometimes they served jail time for their convictions. Chris' mom reflects back to her parenting days and admits that if she would have known what she knows now—what she sees in our family's homeschool—she would have chosen it for him, too. It just wasn't a choice back then.

I suppose you can say *we* are pioneers in childbearing. Though we haven't spent time in jail, we've certainly felt ostracized from folks who wonder why we push back so hard against "normality." There are some who think our pioneering is a fad of sorts, triggered by charismatic crusaders who lead their gullible followers to conformity. They see the strange life we live and wonder, "Perhaps they read a book or something." If you want to see conformity, go to a PTA meeting. If you want to see diversity, go to a homeschool conference, hang out with a group of midwives, or attend a church with four times more children than adults. You'll get opinions that are light-years apart from each other. While public schools have to force feed lessons on "celebrating diversity," it's the status quo in communities like ours. We may be abnormal, but we are far from conformers.

What is there to appreciate about conformity, anyway? Do any of us really think we'll lie back on our deathbeds and ponder, "So glad we were just like our neighbors"? The deathbeds of parents who welcomed children as blessings will be surrounded with a rich and diverse heritage. The childless do not share in this fortune, and one of the saddest realities of our modern world is that most of the childless are so by choice.

A relative was concerned about the challenges we make to parents in this book. "Consider those who are barren," he said. "I'd hate for them to think they are being judged." We're surprised when people think that we would be so thoughtless. Encouraging parents to have children is not close to judging those who aren't physically able. Instead, our focus is on those 20-somethings who voluntarily throw their fertile years away thinking they are making wise, responsible choices. If anything, their perspective turns the stomachs of those who are not able to have children yet desperately desire so.

Much more often than not, intentionally avoiding children is voluntarily checking out from a big chunk of life—to the detriment of yourself, your spouse and the one or two children you do end up having. The mentality of avoiding the blessings walks side by side with the mentality of hiring a stand-in. Why wouldn't a mother send her newborn to day care? Or a nanny? Or a baby-sitter? She has to get back to work.

This is good, liberating advice, not to be taken strictly: Go ahead, pay for a meal and don't cook, or hire a maid to take some of the load off. We're asking quite frankly: To what end are you doing these things? If you're doing them to save some time, ask yourself, *Time for what?* To run the rat race at work? To scan eggs for stay-at-home moms?

Take into consideration all that needs to happen to return to work. Professional clothes, the latest hairdo, makeup, day care, a dependable car, and so on. Studies have been done that show mothers working for mere pennies per hour. Add to that the time, energy, stress and sacrifice required to hold a full-time job, I ask these mothers, "How do you do it?" A better question would be, *Why do you do it?* To work out at the gym?

I played the rat race game years ago and desire never to return. While my school and society at large encouraged me to shake the chains of a patriarchal society, I secretly dreaded the challenge, as I believe most women do. As a single mother, I would get up early, dress and feed my two children and myself, and run out the door to drop them at day care and school to make sure I punched in at work on time. I'd work all day with an assembly line of women all doing the same thing, living the same exact life. Returning home would be just as tumultuous as leaving in the morning: Feed the kids, help with homework, bathe and tuck them in bed. Psychologists (working mothers, no doubt) tout the idea that busy parents like me should focus on "quality" time rather than "quantity" time. What hogwash. What I would have given—back then—for a few good days of nothing to plan for or worry about. In the rat race, there is neither quality nor quantity time. It's hardly a life I'd recommend to anyone.

It was a full life, but not a happy one. I was busy and stressed, and I didn't have a husband to bounce things off of. I was tired, my kids were distressed, and I was alone. Single parenting is the toughest job in the world, and I marvel at those who voluntarily choose it. I speak from experience; I've been there, done that.

I get boiling mad at the media for glamorizing the life of single motherhood. Rock stars flaunt their out-of-wedlock parenting as no big deal, inevitably inspiring young girls to bring children into the world. Mind you, these stars are millionaires who can hire a dozen stand-ins all day and every day. Not so for the 16-year-old high school girl. Life for her is tough, and shame on those in the limelight for making it out to be a great life, when really it's a race that exhausts you.

Here's a bigger marvel: married couples who volunteer for the rat race. Perhaps it's ignorance. The mother and father are simply expected to have a couple of kids and a couple of incomes, send the kids to school and continue to live a self-absorbed life separate from any of the genuine, heartfelt demands of parenting. They don't have another child because they've never thought of having a third (or a fourth or a fifth or a sixth). The years flick by in a blur, and they're hardly aware of the opportunity lost, the great blessing these additional children could have been. They say ignorance is bliss, but is conformity?

We are not looking for stand-ins, and we aren't looking to check out of our parenting roles. If conformity is the societal norm, we want nothing of it. God gave us these children and we have Him to please (and give account), not the cultural authorities or anyone else. We desire our Lord's blessing, "Well done, good and faithful servant" (Matthew 25:21). So we "run in such a way as to get the prize" (1 Corinthians 9:24).

Boy, does this message infuriate conformists! Mothers who do what's expected—chasing career and fortune—grit their teeth at moms who jump out of the cage. They typically embrace the feminist mantras that promise fulfillment both in the home and away at work. Such claims are decades old and as empty as climate change and overpopulation. Couples waste years of their lives, never able to recapture them.

It's sad. As the bumper sticker slogan says, "Even if you win the rat race, you're still a rat."

Like the Walmart checkout lady, you may find these ideas heavy. But don't shake them off. Consider, what would you trade to be the one who takes care of your child? For us, we would trade *everything*, especially a minimum wage job. We love being there to snuggle and read books to them. We're there for the boo-boos and first steps and meals. We don't wait for school plays or soccer tournaments for a chance to see the development of our children. We see it every day, every hour in the Jeub home.

Keep these things in mind the next time your 2-year-old is sick. Wipe her sweet red cheeks and clean up her messes. She sees her mother, not a stand-in. You won't ever look back on this time with guilt or regret. Your children will grow up knowing their mother wasn't checked out, pouring her life into others who meant nothing to your family. They will walk confidently into life knowing that their parents love them, gave their life for them and passed on to them a strong, vigorous heritage.

10 - Heritage

"An harvest of the best, what needs he more?" —Anne
Bradstreet, a mother of eight who was born in 1612

Here we are at the end of our book. We hope you have found encouragement to press on with your convictions, along with a freedom and love that surpasses anything else life can offer. A mom and dad who embrace the commitment to love another child is a couple at the precipice of an exciting life. We can't imagine a more adventurous one.

We have lots of children and we look forward to more before our fertile years are over. We're dabbling now in grandparenting (our second grandchild was born last summer), which is an awesome adventure worth another book! Life keeps chugging along, with nary a boring moment. We have no time to fake our lives, cover up petty sins, pretend to be something we are not. How in the world we were able to pull off this book amidst all the hustle and bustle of life is a miracle itself.

Truth be told, we contemplated not publishing this book at all—or at least waiting a few more years. Because even with more experience under our belts than a half-dozen other more "normal" families, we still feel unprepared some days—inadequate, overwhelmed, inexperienced. Like most parents, we're raising our children the best way we know how, but we're learning as we go. We seek out wisdom from other families, we take (and leave) advice, we succeed with some of our ideas and fail with others. We sometimes ask God, "Are You sure You want *us* to be speaking out about *loving another child?*"

We suppose He does, because we can't shake our desire. The calling to love another child is our heartfelt conviction. God is in control of our family, every aspect of it. There is no room for counterfeit. Our family grows with beautiful new human beings joining it, their personalities touching the lives of everyone around them. They contribute to society and the greater economy, and life goes on. Sometimes we feel we are on a roller coaster, but like kids standing in line again and again for their chance to ride, we jump on. The thrill never gets old.

Some suppose that following God's will for your life will bring persecution, but for us "persecution" hasn't been that bad at all. Sure, we have some who ridicule us on TV gossip sites, but who cares? While there may be a culture that questions our motives, and some in the media may enjoy demonizing our nonprogressive lifestyle, we press on with the confidence and courage necessary to seriously grapple with the countercultural convictions God places on our hearts. We have little choice, really. To complain of persecution is like a millionaire complaining of how tough being rich is. The millionaire, actually, would have the winning argument.

We remember feeling awkward when we started homeschooling in the early '90s. The movement was just beginning to take shape. We were among thousands of parents so displeased with the status quo of education that taking the reins and doing it ourselves became a viable option. I (Chris) had started my teaching career in the public schools right around the time we decided to educate our own children at home, so naturally I expected "persecution." Regardless, I pressed on and tried to be the best teacher I could be.

You know something? The persecution wasn't nearly as bad as I thought it might be. Sure, I had a couple of those union types who got in my face about how nutty I was, but their judgment mattered little. They weren't the good teachers I respected anyway. Most in the educational establishment at the time were genuine teachers who had a heart for educating kids. I found these teachers and administrators more curious than critical, interested in this "new educational choice" called homeschooling.

Today, home education is not so new anymore. It has become a natural and accepted form of educating children. It is so much easier today to homeschool than it was 20 years ago because, really, it isn't so abnormal anymore. Don't be fooled: It's challenging, a serious commitment and a life-altering change to consider. But there's a whole world of home educators out there—many in the same boat as you—with support networks and resources ready to make your homeschool successful.

The years go by and we look back on our anxiety and think, *That wasn't so bad.* This same feeling comes with every conviction we feel God prodding us with. Only a few years ago, we felt the temptation to dip deep into our home equity to build a garage for our vehicles, but God never let us get comfortable with the idea. While most others were spending the equity they had in their homes, we felt it wasn't right. The downsides of debt and our desire to get out from under it were greater than our desire to have a detached garage. We still don't have that garage, but our house is worth more than our mortgage, and not many of our friends can claim that today. In the end, not having a garage isn't all that bad.

We try our best to encourage parents who struggle with the idea of another child, but sometimes we grow impatient with the all-too-common excuse of *persecution.* Typical stories of in-laws making snide comments, neighbors thinking they're weird, getting judgmental stares at the grocery store, etc. Yeah, yeah, yeah. Trust us, we've been through all of that and more. But is this *persecution*? Whenever you trust in God, you will be judged by others. Is it ever not the case? The blessings that flow from our walk with God are too great for us to even consider denying our walk with Him.

Our hesitation to publish this book was a hesitation prompted by fear. We fear exposing our personal conviction to love another child. We know that many people will not understand, grow frustrated with us or even angrily confront us. We already silently suffer through the nosey comments from neighbors, co-workers, church members, etc. And we know that such confrontations will surely increase if we get more vocal about our lives. Judgment already exists for large families like ours, and we're likely going to get it right in the nose when folks start reading this. We're not completely immune! Judgment like this hurts.

Perhaps it is technically *persecution* to be judged for following God's conviction and having another child. But we must keep it in perspective: This is light-years from martyrdom. Our life is filled with unfettered, nonstop, compounded joy. This joy is the direct consequence of having so many blessings running around the house, which is, frankly, a direct result of following our personal convictions. Let the judgments come; our hearts are free. You know what would be a true downer? Living with a house empty of blessings, knowing full well that God had been calling us to something bigger, something better than the status quo. What a cursed existence to wonder what it would have been like if we had the kind of faith God wanted us to have.

Here's a revealing truth: We don't believe parenting is a life of persecution at all. We'll be judged, sure. We face individual snobs (more on that in a little bit), but we are not persecuted. When we venture into Walmart with a dozen-plus kids in tow, without exception we get asked if they are all ours. Daring ones ask us more valuable questions like how we manage them all, how we feed them, etc. This gives us an opportunity to be transparent and share honest answers. People don't really look down on big families. They're just curious. We're more than happy to share our experiences, how we manage to make it all work. And we get most excited when we talk about God's convictions, because we marvel at how His will always turns out to be the best for our lives. God's calling for you—how He convicts you personally—is what's important.

Conviction is a beautiful concept for followers of Christ. Our personal conviction to obey God allows Him to bless us with children. Here's the kicker: Parents who are most concerned with how we handle persecution are typically parents who wrestle with the same convictions we have. Our advice is as simple as the advice reinforced throughout scripture: Choose life (Deuteronomy 30:19). When the negative comments start trickling in, ignore them. Continue on with what God lays on your heart. It's not much more complicated than that. Besides, those negative comments are likely coming from ignorance, and perhaps even envy. Never give negativity root in your life. You're too busy raising your children, taking care of your heritage.

There really is no criticism that can penetrate genuine godly conviction. God is love (1 John 4:16). He loves you and me. And He *convicts* us to follow His calling. What's so bothersome about that? The only bother is when we listen to the presumption—the so-called *culture*, the status quo, the normal or expected ways—about how we should look and act and live. If we all listened to the culture, we would have no leaders, no innovation, no heroes, no progress. Do you really want the life of the ordinary? Is that what you're called to be?

As for the Jeub home, we will walk in God's path,[23] even if it means walking into condemnation from others. The snippy comment from a gossiper rolls off our backs, and they should roll off of yours, too.

Community

If you've ever visited our Web site, you've seen that it is more than just a family blog, though it may appear to be so on the surface.[24] It is a place we hope parents find encouragement. We all have our low times, so we feel the need to stick together and encourage one another. Our blog attracts families who have the same calling to love another child as we do, and when we are able, we post ideas and thoughts that we know will touch the hearts of other couples.

There are so many families who, like us, are walking the walk, dealing the best they can with complex relationships, striving to love one another and seeking God's plan for their lives. We marvel at how some of our guests' posts are so similar to our own thoughts. We learn and reflect and grow from the community that comments on our site.

Some of the posts are hilarious, and we find encouragement in the responses. We posted on how negative responses tend to stop after the seventh child is born, something we referred to earlier in this book. A visitor commented, "Oh, so that's the ticket; I have to have 3 or 4 more before my mom stops asking when I'm done. LOL! I love it!" When we admitted that "hunting for food" was a lame excuse for spending an awful lot of money to play in the woods, somebody wrote, "I'm glad *someone* finally came out and said that hunting isn't very cost effective." It was posted by the adult son of one of my hunting friends, a young dad of three children after three years of marriage. That made us laugh!

The community shares pains, too. It isn't uncommon for families to pour out their hearts and frustrations over having and raising children. We often advise parents to let negative thoughts "roll off their backs," but we know, at times, they hurt. Relationships— though rewarding—can be tough. It may sound mystical, but embracing the pain is sometimes the answer. Great truths that can change your life are often embedded within pain, and God wants us to share those treasures together. Sharing with one another the real pains of family life (prodigals, divorce, ridicule, what have you) often turn you into better parents, better people.

It isn't surprising to see a community of parents form around loving more children. Our personal conviction is quite common: Have children, open your heart to the idea of several children and let God's love pour in to lead you toward a blessed heritage. There is no slick marketing campaign funded by some huge subsidy or led by an underlying denomination or theology. It is as simple as this: God is pressing on parents' hearts to *love another child*.

We covered this, but it bears repeating: If there's a biblical principle we can't miss on it's this: *Love God and love others*. This is the Greatest Commandment. Jesus didn't budge on love. He seldom pointed to theological positions or disputed issues of the day, and never at the expense of love. Instead, He hit the heart of faith itself: "Love God and love others as yourself. This is the greatest commandment. All the law of the prophets hang on these two commandments."

This is what church is: a community of people coming together and loving God and loving one another. We gather in each other's homes (Acts 2:46), pray for one another (James 5:16), share what is going on in our lives (Acts 14:27), and bear one another's burdens

(Galatians 6:2). All of these are acts of love and kindness in a gathered group of people. Such a community is "fulfilling the law of Christ."

When children come into these communities, their homes come alive! Where the love of Christ is present, children fit so neatly, so perfectly. Much like children blessing the economy at large (remember our points earlier), so they bless the smaller economy— the community, neighborhoods, churches, extended families.

Children are full of joy and hope. They have so much future to look forward to. In Matthew 19:13-15, Jesus welcomed little children. When people brought children to Him, "the disciples rebuked those who brought them." The rebuke was turned back on them, however, as Christ said, "Let the little children come to me, and do not hinder them, for the kingdom of heaven belongs to such as these."

Little children? The kingdom of heaven? These are reassuring words from the Son of God to all parents considering another child. But parents who are wrestling with the conviction to have and love children also need support from their church. And that's sometimes harder to get than Jesus' support. Isn't it peculiar how similar churches are to the disciples? We receive letters and e-mails from parents who choose to tell us *first*—not their church—of their news that they're expecting another child. We shower them with encouragement and support. More often than not, their pastors will wrinkle their noses and join in the world's response: "Seriously! *Another child?*"

We believe this stems not only from an incorrect view of the blessing of children, but a skewed perspective of love. We can't let the world become more vocal about love than we are. John Lennon pounded out the premise that "All You Need Is Love." Lenny Kravitz yelled out, "You've Got to Let Love Rule." While we ragged on rock stars in the last chapter, we have to appreciate their desire to have children. How many modern churches are filled with young couples who are waiting to have children, even considering never having any? The church can't and shouldn't cede love to rock stars. If anything is a sign of a lost generation, that would be it.

Communities of Christ-following families (which is what the church is) should *own* the message of the Greatest Commandment. Without love we are not the church. We should, as the popular saying goes, "get right with God." We don't mean getting right by following a list of legalistic rules that have little or nothing to do with loving God and others. We mean getting right with love. "Whoever does not love does not know God, because God is love" (1 John 4:8). God and love are inseparable.

Are we being bullies? We don't think so. We're not expecting too much when we expect people—families and churches included—to love one another. Why would we be interested in communities who think love is frivolous or unimportant? It's the same with our politics. We make no secret about the fact that we're conservative to the core. That said, take love out of our conservative politics and all you've got left are angry jerks. Some of our closest relatives are diehard liberal Democrats … and we love them to death. They may be politically *wrong*, but when we get together for weddings, reunions, even funerals, we have a ball together. If we're daring, we broach the subject of politics and dive into the most heated discussions. But at the end our love is greater than our differences. We're family, and this is the way it should be.

The kids bought me a T-shirt for Father's Day a few years back. Stick figures representing all my kids were stacked up on the front. The slogan read, "World domination, one child at a time." Tongue-in-cheek, to be sure, but embedded in it is a subtle truth. There may be those who think we're having children to take over the world politically or economically, but it has everything to do with the love of Christ. Love must be the foundation for all our macro and micro communities—familial, political, religious, economical. Without love, we are needlessly nihilist or mindlessly fanatical.

Walking with God is the most exciting life journey to choose, and followers of Christ are the ones who will be countercultural and revolutionary. It's easy to deny Christ and walk alongside the world. Parents who do not know Jesus Christ will conform to the expectations of our society (and therefore have only a few children, if any at all). The mandate of the Church is quite the opposite:

"Do not conform any longer to the pattern of this world, but be transformed by the renewing of your mind. Then you will be able to test and approve what God's will is—his good, pleasing and perfect will" (Romans 12:2). Left with the choice of the well-trod path of the world's and the less-traveled walk of Christ, we opt for the walk of Christ.

We aren't consumed with populist prospects; we're focused on love. Though others may refuse children; we say, "Let them come" (Matthew 19:14). We are parents of 15-going-on-16 children who have grown to believe love is "the most excellent way" (1 Corinthians 12:31) to raise a family. Our world should be all about love that fills communities to overflowing. Married couples—and siblings, extended family, children and adults alike—should consume their thoughts with love.

It starts in our homes, "one child at a time." Love in the house must never be compromised. Families and communities who focus on love first and foremost are those that prosper, and children fit that prosperity quite nicely. Christ is at home in these families of faith, children are welcomed and parents are encouraged to love another child. Why not? Love multiplies and life's challenges are overcome.

We love this life journey. Love another child? You bet! And we know that there are countless other couples who feel the same way. They know in their hearts that children are blessings. Despite the world's best arguments, they have a love beating in their hearts to love another child, perhaps many more. We believe this is God working, calling them to let the children come, to embrace the truth of Christ. It's exciting and beautiful and free. Enjoy the life. *Love another child.*

notes

¹ Jim Bob and Michelle Duggar are featured with their now-19 children on their own show on TLC. They have received ridicule from some viewers, but their show is still extremely popular. In our opinion, the Duggars are great people who follow their convictions confidently, and their family is beautiful.

² Our ministry, Training Minds Ministry, is built largely on the verse 1 Peter 3:15, which reads, in part, "Always be prepared to give a reason for the hope that you have."

³ To view the show in its entirety, visit the iTunes Store and do a search. The cost for the entire 1-hour show is only a couple of dollars.

⁴ "Our View." The Colorado Springs Gazette. March 20, 2008. http://www.gazette.com/opinion/friday-34451-victims-view.html

⁵ Lila Rose, a former student of the homeschool league our home business provides for, used her speaking skills to conduct sting operations on abortion clinics. In her debut video, she posed as a 14-year-old girl whose 34-year-old boyfriend told her to get an abortion. See www.liveaction.org.

⁶ It is no secret that Planned Parenthood is the leading distributor of contraception in the world. Despite its almost-certain failure rates, the organization still promotes sexual promiscuity.

⁷ Partial birth abortion occurs in the last trimester of a pregnancy. The procedure is exactly as its name denotes: The baby is induced

and partially born before the doctor cuts the spinal cord and kills the child.

[8] Ehrlich, Paul. *The Population Bomb.* Sierra Club-Ballantine Books. 1968.

[9] You can still read the article from 1975 here at http://www.denisdutton.com/cooling_world.htm.

[11] The media brought light to these comments by the United State's two most powerful men. If you missed these two stories, do a quick Google search.

[12] A recent (2007) movie that exposes many of the problems with the modern birthing industry is *The Business of Being Born.* Visit http://www.thebusinessofbeingborn.com for more.

[13] *Husband-Coached Childbirth: The Bradley Method of Natural Childbirth,* by Robert A. Bradley, Marjie Hathaway, Jay Hathaway, James Hathaway. Random House, Inc., 2008.

[14] From *The Bradley Method*, the method of child delivery we practice. This Web site has a wealth of information for you to research: http://www.bradleybirth.com.

[15] Vitamins are hardly ever prescribed, but studies show that vitamin D helps prevent preeclampsia (http://prenatal-health.suite101.com/article.cfm/pregnancy_nutrition_and_preeclampsia).

[16] If weight is an issue for you as a mother, we refer you to *Love in a Diet,* by Wendy Jeub.

[17] Susan McCutcheon-Rosegg. *Natural Childbirth the Bradley Way.* Plum Publishing. Rev. ed. 1996.

[18] This information usually shocks people, but think about it: who's telling you to play it safe at the hospital? The hospital. Do the proper research and you'll find home birth to be a more viable option than not (http://www.gentlebirth.org/format/myths.html).